ORGANISATION OF SCHOOL EDUCATION

About the Author

Mohit Chakrabarti teaches Education and English at Visva-Bharati University, Santiniketan, India 731235. Regularly participates and presents papers in National conferences, seminars, symposia, workshops etc. Significant participation/presentation/ acceptance of papers in the World Assembly of Teacher-Educators, the University of the West Indies, Kingston, Jamaica, 1986; Beijing Normal University, Beijing. People's Republic of China. 1989; The Institute of Education, Singapore. 1990.

A poet, translator, book-reviewer and critic, profusely writes in many periodicals and research journals of repute.

A prolific writer for children in English and Bengali. Credited with ample creative and critical contributions.

Member, International Council for Education and Teaching, Virginia, U.S.A.

Professional Member, Centre for Advanced Study in Education and Management Training Research, Hyderabad, India.

Recipient of National Award as a Teacher-Educator.

A consistent and devoted contributor to studies in Rabindranath Tagore's educational thoughts and experiments and Gandhian scholar.

Books by the same author from Concept:

Gandhian Humanism
Gandhian Spiritualism
Pioneers in Philosophy of Education

ORGANISATION OF SCHOOL EDUCATION
Prospects, Problems and Planning

MOHIT CHAKRABARTI
Professor of Education
Visva - Bharati University
Santiniketan

CONCEPT PUBLISHING COMPANY, NEW DELHI - 110059

ISBN 81-7022-594-9 (H.B.)

First Published 1997

Published and Printed by
Ashok Kumar Mittal
Concept Publishing Company
A/15-16, Commercial Block, Mohan Garden
New Delhi-110059 (India)
Phones : 5504042, 5554042

TO
MY MOTHER

PREFACE

Education is always a beckoning and a challenge. Organisation of School education is more challenging and thrilling because it is concerned with children who are global citizens of future.

To organise the school as a centre for community living is yet a challenging and crucial task. This essentially calls forth redesigning the school climate in a democratic set-up where parents, teachers and pupils along with the community representatives make a happy fusion of theories and concepts of education in practice in a joyous and living atmosphere of learning.

The advancement of learning of the child does not altogether depend on teaching in class-rooms nor does it depend on mutual reactions between the learner and the teacher alone, but on a joint endeavour made by teachers, parents and learners in particular. Hence, the importance of better re-organisation of co-curricular activities and parent- teacher associations.

Classification of pupils and organised school planning are essential catchment areas of school development. A newer approach to this direction is undeniable. Moreover, organisation of instructional strategies like micro-teaching, questioning and value-orientation necessitate special attention.

If education is primarily meant for promotion of excellence in every individual learner, organisation of education for creative and critical appreciation becomes all the more important. At the same time, organisation of aesthetic education should also be considered for continual and careful exercise of pupils' aesthetic sensibilities. In this connection, the organisational avenues of teaching poetry for acceleration and excellence in aesthetic sensibilities may be explored anew.

Organisation of school education is closely related to the role of the headmaster as an organiser. As such, the prospects and possibilities of revamping his an organisational leadership demand extensive study and research.

I gratefully acknowledge the service of Sri Nemai Chandra Ghosh Bag, Santiniketan, who has prepared the type-script of my manuscript.

If the book appeals to students, teachers and others interested in education and rewards me with their invaluable suggestions for incorporation of newer perspectives of school organisation, I would say aside : 'What a prize!'

Seemantika MOHIT CHAKRABARTI
Seemanto Palli
SANTINIKETAN - 731 235
WEST BENGAL, INDIA

CONTENTS

1

ORGANISING A SCHOOL AS A COMMUNITY SCHOOL

Community Consciousness: A New Dimension

Education, for better emancipation of individuality, should ensure community consciousness. This means that an individual, in order to develop his unique power of individuality and exercise it for the good of one and all, must share the manifold experiences of the community in which he lives and contribute his own reactions to the betterment of the community. Undoubtedly, this is an arduous task to be practised, and prior to practice, it necessitates learning right from the beginning of one's life.

In secondary schools, pupils receive conjoint communicated experiences, a fact John Deway so characteristically points out in his invaluable book *Democracy and Education,* and the seeds of awareness to community life are carefully sown to be nurtured throughout the ongoing stages of life. The individual pupil thus receives an opening for sharing and expressing his own experiences in an ideal atmosphere. His own tastes and temperaments, mood and manners, habits and hobbies undergo orientations implicit or explicit-in an assembly of different dimensions that beckon newer avenues of individual excellence. This is not merely an ideal or a definite course of personal advancement but this also leads to a desirable march for the common good of humanity. That a man becomes 'men' in the community, and the community, on the other hand, becomes a unit of common goodness in every walk of life are the new dimensions yet properly considered and actions undertaken thereto in our secondary education.

The rift of ideas and ideals, the utter indifference to group life, absence of vigorous community activity programmes, lack of regular but cautious incentives to community consciousness—all these prove the fact that whatever education is imparted in the secondary schools in our country fails to imbibe among pupils the spirit of community living and community awareness. Consequently, one cannot but accept the ignoble fact so poignantly expressed by the Education Commission (1964-66), that even now, education is 'bought'. The tragedy reaches its climax when both individual excellence and community consciousness become alien affairs in teaching-learning programmes. What an irony in the name of education? The discovery of education for community consciousness is a definite precondition to eliminate 'buying' education, and this would also lead to emancipation of individuality. Undeniably, it is the responsibility of every secondary school to earnestly chalk out and implement programmes for development of community consciousness among pupils.

Objectives

In order to organise a school as community school, the following objectives might be considered:

(i) to develop a rich community life and, accordingly, to enable pupils to have the same ;

(ii) to provide pupils with adequate opportunities to organise and participate in community programmes ;

(iii) to enable pupils to suggest community programmes of their own and, as far as possible, to transfer them into reality ;

(iv) to train pupils in the use of equipments, instruments and appliances necessary for scientifically negotiating community activity programmes ;

(v) to enable pupils to cultivate the following sincerely :

  (a) sense of aesthetics,
  (b) sense of creativity,
  (c) sense of critical appreciation,
  (d) sense of discipline,
  (e) sense of punctuality,
  (f) sense of morality,
  (g) sense of values,
  (h) sense of scientific approach,
  (i) sense of tolerance and
  (j) sense of unity.

Community Work Programme : Areas of Activities

Every secondary school incorporates within itself different pupils belonging to different communities. It has the common platform of union amongst pupils of diverse race, religion, caste, creed, culture, dress, manners, customs etc. which contribute a lot to the rich heritage and tradition of a multi-dimensional country like India. What is obviously important is to chalk out carefully community programmes so that these enable pupils to have the above mentioned desirable objectives fulfilled or achieved in a worthwhile manner. The following Tables 'A' 'B' and 'C' might signify different areas of community activities to be performed in secondary schools.

TABLE - A : School

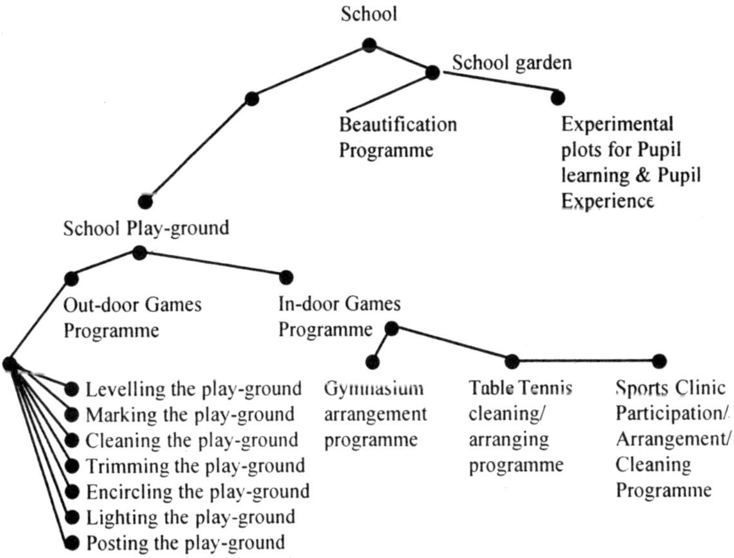

TABLE - B : School : Community Work Programmer

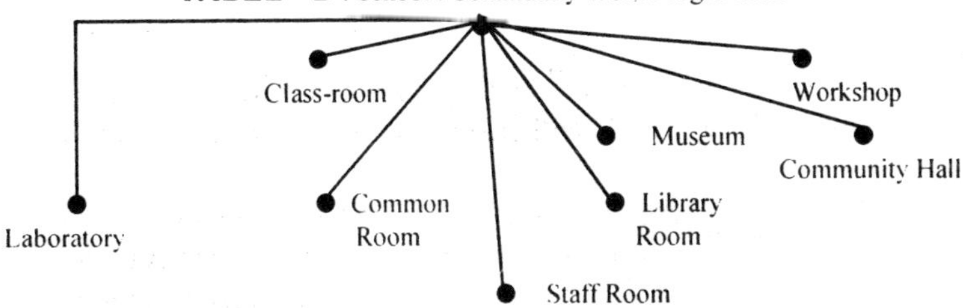

TABLE - C : School

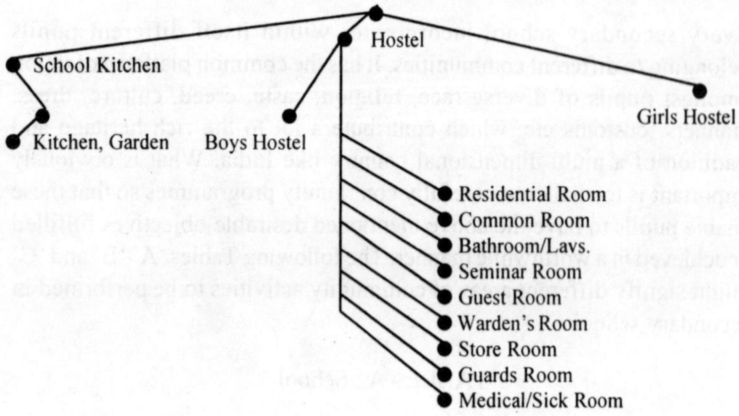

Job Specification And Desirable Outcomes From Different Areas

With the introduction of programmes for community activities in secondary schools, pupils are blessed with the cultivation of manual as well as intellectual, moral, emotional, aesthetic, creative and spiritual exercise. The following are some of the activities that can be introduced through organisation of community work programme in secondary schools:

(i) Cleaning: Class-rooms, play-grounds, hostels, kitchen etc.
(ii) Levelling: Playground, gardens, roads etc.
(iii) Gardening: Spacework, top dressing, manuring, planting etc.
(iv) Decoration: Class-rooms, other instructional rooms, external areas.
(v) Painting: "
(vi) Whitewashing: "
(vii) Sanitation: Bathrooms, drainage systems, water works.
(viii) Work for Aesthetic and Creative Appeal: Installing/placing photos, paper-cutting, dolls, pictures, models, wall-magazines etc.

Undeniably, organisation of the aforementioned community activities in secondary schools will enable pupils to be ensured with the following qualities:

(a) Cleanliness, (b) self-help, (c) devotion to manual work, (d) dignity of labour, (e) sense of equality, (f) unity, (g) perseverance, (h) discipline, (i) follow-feeling, (j) punctuality and (k) co-operation.

The above are some of the essential qualities attained through organisation of community work, which are a pointer to further advancement of manhood. Moreover, with added interest imbibed through association with teachers in charge of administration, organisation and supervision of pupil-activities, students themselves gladly accept all responsibilities and find joy and thrill in working in a group or working alone. A sense of togetherness coupled with a sense of beauty in work enable each pupil to discover newer avenues of community activities and to chalk out planned schedules of activities accordingly. With occasional advice and suggestions from the teachers concerned, "every work", to educate in the words of Ruskin, " turns into worship" , we allow our pupils to be spirited in the worship of God through worship in work.

Moreover, launching of community work outside the school campus can also be introduced, and organisation of the following activities needs priorities in the context of appalling social and emotional imbalance and disintegration:

(a) Organisation of public health and sanitation programmes.
(b) Looking after the old/infirm/children.
(c) Solving problems of social ills.
(d) Helping the sick and nursing them.
(e) Eradicating malnutrition.
(f) Launching literary programmes.
(g) Re-constructing vital road-links.
(h) Conducting games and sports.
(i) Conducting recreational programmes.

Towards a Newer Beginning

That education is more than attainment of mere certificates, diplomas, degrees etc. can hardly be ignored. In a rapidly changing world, education is continually having a newer connotation. A newer beginning in all our educational activities is not only a promise in theory but also one to be performed in right earnest. The hope of regeneration of mankind out of rampant devaluation of values lies in sincerely infusing the spirit of service to the community concerned to every young learner in our secondary schools. And who but teachers would whole-heartedly accept this ardent assignment?

2

REDESIGNING THE SCHOOL CLIMATE

Education is always dependent on good schooling. It may either be self-schooling or schooling in the form of advancement of learning by means of educational institutions as prevalent everywhere. Undeniably, the best type of schooling is self-schooling where the school climate is self-designed and self-guided, self-administered and self-improved but, then, such a congenial climatic condition as designed within is rarely available due to manifold reasons beyond human control. The only alternative for a learner to devote to advancement of learning is the educational institution where he encounters and reacts with the climate favourable or unfavourable.

Today's education in secondary schools, let us frankly admit is confronted with innumerable climatic lapses. Neither physical nor social nor even cultural and aesthetic conditions are in tune with a pupil's urge for making an adventure into the world of knowledge and wisdom, information and experience, exploration and poignance. A four-walled prison house as the school is, it has yet to eliminate its disgraceful conditions in legion which amply contribute to its being what Rabindranath Tagore has most painfully and realistically depicted as *dasta-panchtar Andaman*-the Andaman from ten to five.

Apart from the fact that education has already become a routinized, mechanized, passive, lifeless affair in secondary schools in particular, it has lost its true significance in preparing a learner to be alive to himself as well as to others. It has also lost its ground to serve the learner to discover and maintain the favourable climatic conditions of his growth and development from diverse dimensions.

Three Factors

In order to redesign the school climate, the following three factors necessitate proper attention and maintenance:

(i) The physical factor,
(ii) The social factor and
(iii) The cultural and aesthetic factor.

In case of the physical factor, it is hardly denied that at present most of the secondary schools specially in urban and semi-urban areas suffer from absence of favourable physical climate. Lack of space, undesirable location of the school, negligence of health and hygiene are more or less the regular characteristics associated with the physical climate of urban or semi-urban secondary schools. Under such circumstances, pupils gasp in educational spasm and all the efforts made by teachers in class-rooms or elsewhere embrace failures in non-response. As education never accepts miracles in perfection, it never proves a success in unfavourable climatic conditions of pupil-efflorescence.

The social factors related to the school climate need no elaborate explanation. Today's education in secondary schools in our country in particular suffer from the ills of social abnormalities. A diverse mix-up of social settings like the high and the low, the rich and the poor, the advantaged and the disadvantaged pupils thronging in schools most often heterogeneously gives a sordid picture of absence of cohesion in pupil-climate for educational endeavour and exercise. Pupil-groups lack motivation due to innumerable social reasons that are very delicate and touchy. Even the best efforts at bringing about favourable social climate are proved a failure due to infiltration of the undesirable ideas and sentiments of social disintegration as an off-shoot of bad text books, adverse reflections of social customs and superstitions on pupils in the school and so on. Moreover, social inequalities affect the all-round growth and development of pupils who lack orientation in social ideas and principles of conjoint communicated living in the different school programmes, functions and festivals.

About the defeating roles of cultural and aesthetic factors in secondary schools the less said the better. The most unfortunate part of pupil-progress and pupil-evaluation in secondary schools everywhere indicates these vital factors of pupil-growth and development ignored, misunderstood and averted. A certain lack of exercise in cultural and aesthetic sensibilities leading to appreciation of Truth, Beauty and Goodness in manifold affairs of life has already affected favourable school climate. Consequently, with absence of exercise of love, sympathy, mercy, service, fellow-feeling, co-operation, tolerance, benevolnce etc. that are not only essential but also mandatory for education for fulness, the school climate contributes a little to appreciating pupil-potentiality and pupil-sensibility. Whither education?

The parameters of socio-cultural and socio-aesthetic developments of our learners in secondary schools side by side with physical and aesthetic climate conducive to all round manifestation of excellence and creativity necessitate a re-designed approach that will certainly usher forth a newer avenue of educational development. As a matter of fact, educational planning and administration await an adventure in bringing about favourable school climate to translate pupil-poignance into reality.

The Zenith Points

The zenith points of favourable climatic conditions in secondary schools may be represented as follows:

TABLE - A: The Physical Climate

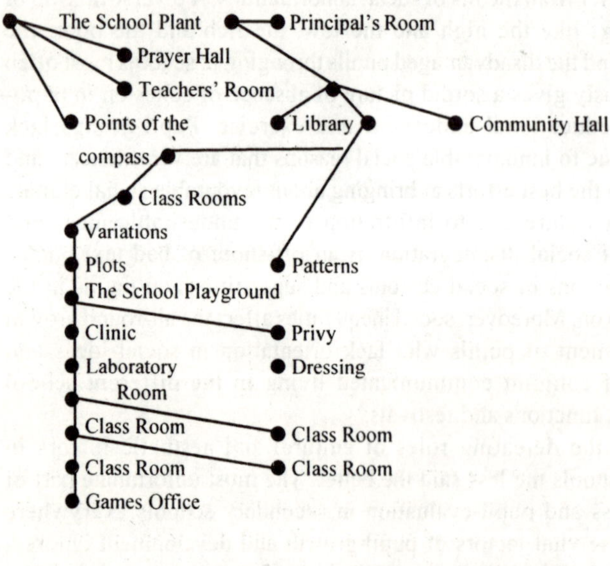

TABLE- B: The Socio-cultural climate

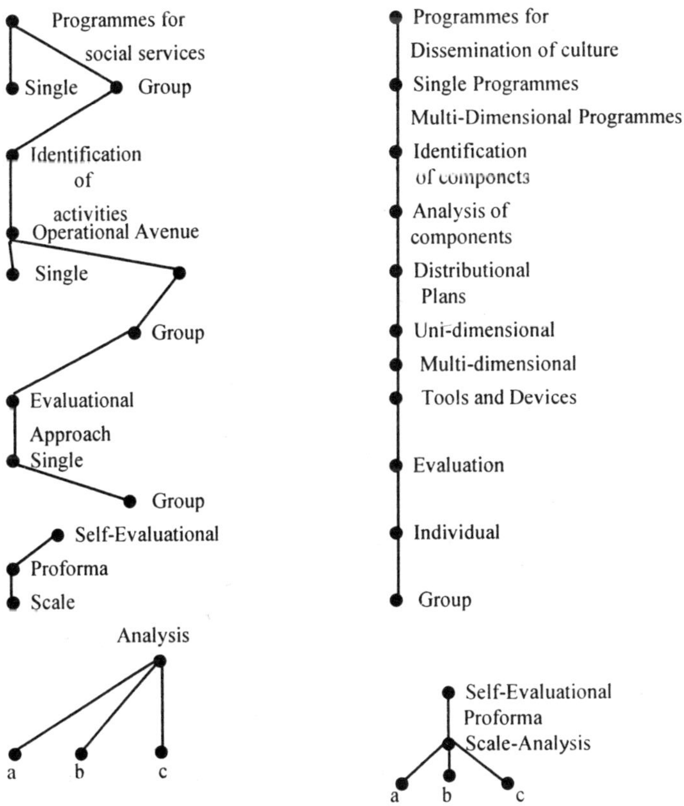

a ● very satisfactory
b ● satisfactory
c ● not satisfactory

TABLE - C: The Social-Aesthetic Climate

Theoretical Programmes
Practical Programmes

Phase I :Identification of components

Phase II : Performance-Avenues

Phase III: Evaluation Schedules

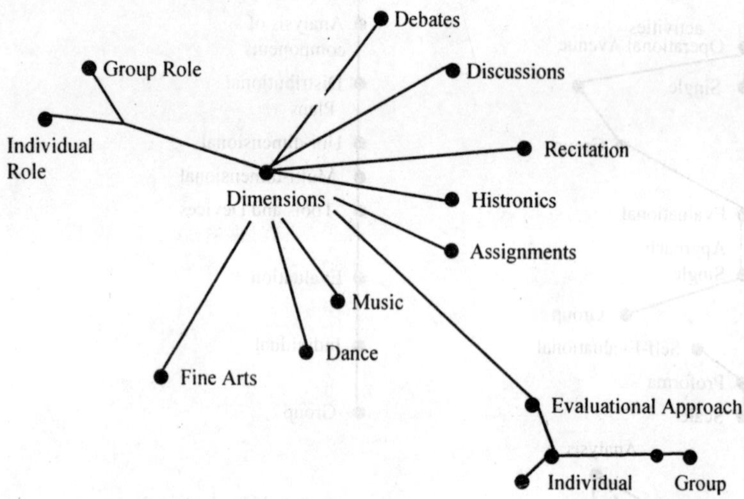

From a study of the Tables A, B and C it is evident that for re-designing the school climate what is of primary importance is to introduce a radical approach to planning and administration in secondary schools.

As for redesigning the physical climate, steps should be taken to see that it is in keeping with the funds available or likely to be available in near future. A highly ambitious plan of re-designing the physical climate of the school ignoring availability or non-availability of funds and resource materials cannot but embrace frustration and failure. In fact, most of the secondary schools fight shy of this truth. Advice in this connection should be sought from eminent educational thinkers, school planners and architects and organisations like the National Council of Educational Research and Training (NCERT) and the National Institute of Educational Planning and Administration NIEPA). In fact, the expert opinions of the NCERT and the NIEPA might steer us towards new horizons of redesigning the physical climate of a secondary school. The multi-purpose use of the class-rooms, community hall, library, games and sports unit, prayer hall, or the administrative buildings of the school require a well-planned programme of survey work and consultation with expert personnels.

With regard to advancement of the socio-cultural climate of the school, care should be taken to promote individual as well as group endeavour in the dissemination of social and cultural harmony. Identification of social and cultural components leading to development of the spirit of oneness is to be made both individually and in groups by pupils and the teachers concerned must take significant roles to initiate pupils from time to time. In this connection, it should be remembered that the teachers themselves should set examples through direct involvements in such socio-cultural programmes, if necessary.

Care should also be taken to see that the socio-aesthetic climate is never marred by emotional outbursts and over enthusiasm. A certain sense of restraint in tone and temperament in handling socio-aesthtic programmes of activities is not only necessary but perhaps obligatory.

Class-room decorations with flowers and foliage, arrangements of flower vases with bouquets, redesigning the class room with *alpanas* pictures, art matters, knitting and fresco work etc. signify appropriate aesthetic and social appeal. Maintenance of neatness all around the school campus and introducing school beautification programmes with activities like cleanliness and gardening have their farflung appeal to the society everywhere.

For a Journey Anew

What we essentially need in redesigning the school climate is to undertake a journey anew to meet the hopes and aspirations of millions of our country. The challenge that we face in such redesigning is the crucial challenge of education that rightly demands our seriousness of purpose as follows:

> In the light of the fundamental role assigned to education in national well - being and development, it is necessary to decide as to how resource will be allocated for education and the extent to which Central Government would assume the responsibility to promote priority programmes and how possibly, the share of education might be augmented within the framework of completing demands in different status. It is essential that qualitative, quantitative and temporal objectives should be determined through an iterative process with reference to the availability of resources. Otherwise adoption of indisputably unimplementable targets results in disorientation, ad-hocism and lack of commitment.
>
> — *Challenge of education—A Policy Perspective.* Ministry of Education, Government of India, New Delhi August 1985, p.65.

Are we aware?

3

ACCELERATING BETTER SCHOOL-COMMUNITY RELATIONSHIP IN SECONDARY SCHOOLS

School education today is undergoing severe stress and strain. The relationship between the school and the community is, let us frankly admit, far from being satisfactory. As a consequence, school participation in community programmes and *vice versa* are few and far between. A 'conjoint communicated experience' no longer exists in the splattered outcome of education. A denial to the above concept of communicating and democratic education highlighted by none else than John Deway is a denial of human manifestation towards the right direction. Hence, acceleration of better school-community relationship.

Objectives

The aims and objectives of accelerating better school-community relationship in secondary schools may be spelt out as follows:

1. To provide ample opportunities for pupils to come in close contact with the community both theoretically and practically and to enable them to spontaneously contribute to acceleration of better school-community relationship.
2. To enable pupils to enjoy community atmosphere in schools.
3. To stimulate pupils to discover newer avenues of better school community relationship and to apply suggestive measures thereof.
4. To boost pupil-participation in community programmes undertaken from time to time.

5. To develop the sense of leadership among pupils in sharing and organising activities in connexion with promotion of school-community relationship.
6. To encourage pupils in bringing out pamphlets, journals, magazines, leaflets of their own devoted to the betterment of school-community relationship.
7. To guide pupils in organising programmes of their own earmarked for promotion of school-community relationship.
8. To foster in pupils the essential components of school-community relationship leading to good citizenship.
9. To enkindle the spirit of better community consciousness among pupils.
10. To allow pupils to be ensured with the evaluational avenues of school-community relationship.

Operational Strategies

The operational strategies for accelerating better school-community relationship in secondary schools necessitate accurate identification and analysis. Therefore, all programmes encompassing betterment of school-community relationship should be carefully chalked out and organised and occasional scrutinies both theoretical and practical should be cautiously carried out.

In undertaking any programme for betterment of school-community relationship in secondary schools, the following schedule of activities should be carried out in order:—

(i) Survey of the programme of activities.
(ii) Planning of the programmes.
(iii) Execution of the programme.
(iv) Evaluation of the programme.
(v) Post evaluational activities in connection with the programmes already carried out.

While making an endeavour to sincerely accomplish the above, care should be taken to negotiate the following:

(i) Adjustability to the school time-table.
(ii) Feasibility of the programme of work.
(iii) Community acceptability of the programme.
(iv) Community co-operational avenues.
(v) Pupil-attitude to and pupil-interest in the programme.

(vi) Appropriate teaching personnels.
(vii) Appropriate community representatives sharing a common concern for betterment of school-community relationship.
(viii) Assistance, if needed, of any other agencies.
(ix) Operation aids: their quality and availability in time.
(x) Framing proper and easy-to-be-administered evaluation-tools.

For better operational strategies in encouraging better school-community relationship, programmes may be undertaken from two-fold avenues:

(a) Long-term programmes.
(b) Short-term programmes.

But, in any case, spelling out every programme appropriately and scientifically is mandatory. Moreover, any switch-over from one programme to the other should pre-suppose and ensure continuity.

In secondary schools, community activities may be geared to the following:

(i) Construction and/or repair of roads, stands etc.
(ii) Eradication of illiteracy.
(iii) Community health programme.
(iv) Caressing the distressed children of the community
(v) Looking after the old and the infirm.
(vi) Serving the physically disadvantaged.
(vii) Helping the poor and needy people.
(viii) Raising funds for the common welfare of the community.
(ix) Encouraging better farming and horticulture.
(x) Launching programmes for communal and national harmony.

The above operational areas of activities are not exhaustive but suggestive, and any community activity programme should be oriented towards furtherance of community consciousness and group cohesion.

Evaluational Avenues

To make any programme for betterment of school-community relationship successful, the evaluational avenues are to be clearly spelt out. This will also indicate the follow-up programmes for each and every pupil to be undertaken. Moreover, both the teacher and the pupil become more interested in sincere endeavour to every community work item.

The following is an Evaluation Card for pupils participating in Community Work Programmes, which might be considered for recording and accelerating community consciousness:

EVALUATION RECORD CARD

I. Name of the pupil...
Class......................Section.......................Roll No...........................
Sex................Age.................................Session: 1st
2nd
3rd
Date....................Time......................Period (s) covered..................
Name of the teacher/guide............................

II. Work-schedule
Type of work undertaken...
Date....................................
Initial informatics........A brief survey:
....
....
....
Time devoted.............................
Teacher's/Guide's remarks:
....
....
....
....

III. Self-evaluation by the pupil :
Do you like the programme? Yes
To some extent
Not at all
What are the areas of the work schedule that you like most? (a) ....
(b) ....
(c) ....
Your suggestions for improvement...

****

IV. Remarks of the community representative.......................................
V. Remarks of the Principal ....
....

4

ORGANISING THE SCHOOL FOR DEMOCRATIC LIVING

When education stands for widening of opportunities for the limited few- the privileged ones, – it encompasses everything *sans* democracy. And the oft-quoted definition of democracy that declares government of the people, by the people and for the people, remains altogether abstract and alien for one and all in the true spirit of education. A cautions look at the spread of secondary education in our country right from the dawn of national independence does not give us a glowing picture of democracy imbibed and enjoyed by pupils in right earnest. But instead, pupils even of the same school or to be more specific, of the same class fail to share the experiences of one another. Moreover, the spirit of oneness so ardently expected to be manifested through exercise of the democratic spirit among pupils rarely finds the light of reality.

While education, as the Report of the Education Commission (the Kothari Commission 1964-66) poignantly remarks, can be 'bought' and educational opportunities are butchered to opportunism, democracy almost faces extinction or becomes a mere show in nepotism and suffers from educational disintegration in aims and objectives, in particular. This, then is the tragedy of democracy so ill-nourished from infancy at school-stages and the happy breeding of the germs of class-consciousness in absence of unity and national solidarity is continually shattering our dream of an ideal democratic India.

Objectives

In order to organise the secondary schools for democratic living the following objectives might be considered:

(a) To enable pupils to be inspired with the spirit of fellow-feeling and to serve neighbours to the best of their capacities and efforts.

(b) to enable pupils to be attuned with the spirit of brotherhood by doing away with casteism, parochialism, provincialism or fissiparous tendencies committed to disintegrate and disturb national solidarity.

(c) to equip pupils with devotion to social service, and, in doing so, enable them to be aware of social ills and superstitions that stand in the way of socialism and democracy.

(d) to enable pupils to be conscious of dignity of labour and to fruitfully engage themselves in manual labour with intellectual exercise.

(e) to enable pupils to consolidate their thoughts on service to the society thereby heartily accepting the solemn pledge of service to the nation even in and through self-service for the greater interest of the country.

(f) to enable pupils to be interested in group learning or more particularly in learning through joyous group activities.

Areas of Activities

To translate the true spirit of democracy into reality among pupils in secondary schools, the following areas of activities might be considered for implementation at the early stage:

TABLE - A : Schedule of Activities to be introduced at the early stage:

Sl. No.	Items	Specifications Individual	Group
1.	Reading	"	"
2.	Recitation	"	"
3.	Histrionic Performance	"	"
4.	Interpretation of (i) Models	"	"
	(ii) Charts	"	"
	(iii) Maps	"	"
	(iv) Diagrams		
	(v) Films/Film-strips	"	"
	(vi) Cassette-programmes including performing arts and day-to-day happening of life	"	"

TABLE - B : Schedule of Activities for Organisation of School for Democratic Living

Sl. No.	Name of the Activity	Distribution of work description	Time allotted	Time actually utilized	Time allotted for further orientation and discussion on already intro-duced	Non-Tuitional involvement, if any, with rerasons thereof	Any other organisational aids/ suggestions accepted & introduced	Remarks of Group Leaders	Remarks of individual pupil	Remarks of the teacher incharge	Follow-up programme
1	2	3	4	5	6	7	8	9	10	11	12
		Phase I / Phase II / Phase III Name of activity in part / Total Distribution Pattern / Group Activity Individual Activity Evaluation	Phase I Phase II Phase II	Phase I Phase II Phase II	Phase I Phase II Phase II	Phase I Phase II Phase II	Phase I Phase II Phase II	Phase I Phase II Phase II	Phase I Phase II Phase II	Phase I Phase II Phase II	Phase I Phase II Phase II

With a view to launching the programme of activities for awakening and promotion of the spirit of democracy among our pupils reading in secondary schools in the most scientific, objective, pin-pointed and ever-alert manner, Table B. might be considered:

It might be noted in this connection that any activity whether to be performed individually or in a group might be modelled or re-modelled for better and more effective efforescence of democratic spirit in every pupil.

Special and specific schedules of activities apart from the general ones may be implemented keeping in view a close follow-up programme for elimination of communication and information gaps.

To inculcate the spirit of democracy among our young learners in secondary school is, therefore, a continuous as well as a cautions process that pre-supposes involvement—direct and/or indirect—of a band of devoted teachers, workers and administrators always ready to shoulder any sort of responsibilities. In fact, children hardly disbelieve the sense of the self-sacrifice at the altar of benevolence and sympathy. What is of immediate necessity is a united effort of all neighbouring schools in each area, for instance, to make our students aware of the string of oneness. This will not merely strengthen unity, a so long neglected entity of democracy, so to say, but would enkindle the spirit of democracy inherent in each of them. How long should we march with the show of democracy in romantic fashion?

5

ORGANISING PARENT-TEACHER ASSOCIATIONS IN SECONDARY SCHOOLS

Education is always an experience–joyous, thrilling, pulsating. It always calls forth newer avenues of exploration and adventure. Pupils in secondary schools are by nature buoyant. They await the green signal for a go afresh in learning and exploring newer avenues of knowledge and skill, understanding and appreciation. But the desirable outcome of all these remains a myth.

Admittedly, the parent–teacher relation in secondary schools in our country is hardly cared for not is it organised in an objective–based, scientific and evaluation–oriented pattern. Whatever relation is based or established among the teachers, the parent and the institution is either with the school admission or the school promotion. Apart from that the picture of parent-teacher relationship is rather very sordid and painful. Parents are given notice to negotiate with pupil-indiscipline, pupil-behavioural abnormalities or pupil-transfer. Teachers, on the other hand, also face untoward circumstances consequential to pupil-performances in different types of examination — oral or written. Sometimes teachers also become unfortunate victims to power-polities. Enlarged perhaps becomes the arena of ukase when teaching in a brilliant and qualitative manner becomes a disqualification, which sometimes leads to termination of service due to vested interest. What an irony in the name of education in general and organisation of parent teacher relationship in particular:

Objectives

Keeping in view the above backdrop of education in secondary schools, the objectives of organising parent-teacher associations may by spelt-out as follows:

(i) To enable the secondary school administration to uphold and accelerate the principles and programmes of education in close association with parents and teachers.

(ii) To allow every secondary school to exercise its own strategy for organising the parent-teacher association and launch programmes of activities accordingly.

(iii) To stimulate parents and teachers to meet regularly and discuss on different problems related to pupil-progress and pupil-excellence.

(iv) To encourage such an association to be in close touch with other similar or allied associations for improvement and acceleration of organisational activities.

(v) To enable the association to experiment and to be deeply involved in the latest trends and strategies of pupil-teaching and pupil-excellence.

(vi) To enable the teachers of such an association to frankly open out and submit informatics related to pupils with their parental approaches and find out solutions therefrom.

(vii) To stimulate parents to be sincerely involved in the different programmes of the school.

(viii) To encourage parents to come forward with their invaluable suggestions for improvement of the school in general, and of pupil-progress in particular.

(ix) To evolve newer avenues of implementing instruction in teaching and learning.

(x) To enable the P.T.A. to occasionally hold seminars, conferences, discussions etc. for a better and healthier relationship between the school and the community.

Organising the Parent-Teacher Association : A Model

The areas of activities of the Parent-Teacher Association in a secondary school are legion. For a smooth functioning of the Association, the following model may be suggested:

Part I :
- (i) Publication of the School Bulletin of the Parent-Teacher Association.
- (ii) Spelling out the work schedule.
- (iii) Informing suitable and necessary organisations.

Part II:
- (i) Implementation Procedures of the P.T.A.
- (ii) Evaluation Programmes.
- (iii) Guidance Activities.

Part III: (i) Post-Evaluational Activities of the P.T.A.
(ii) Maintenance of Records.
(iii) Maintenance of Reports.

Work-Analysis of the Parent-Teacher Association

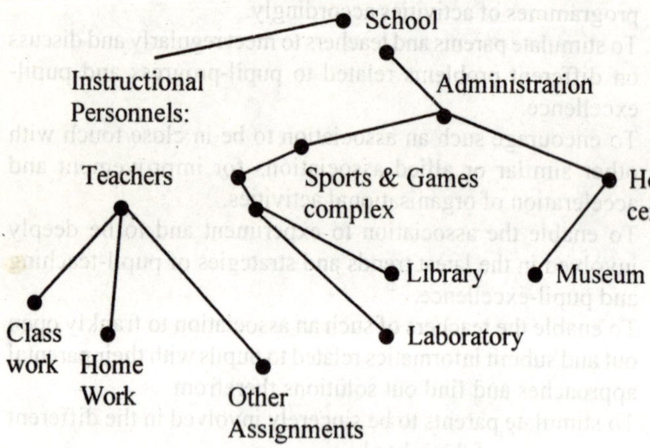

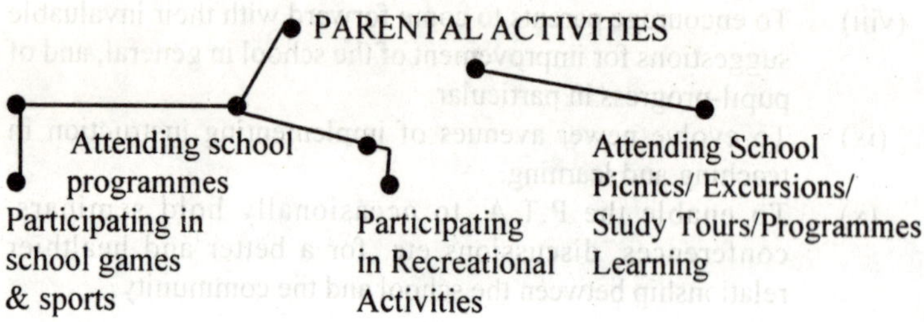

In addition to the above, every secondary school may introduce the following:

(i) The Parent-Teacher Association Journal
(ii) The School Diary for day-to-day Activities
(iii) The Parents' Diary
(iv) The School Suggestion Book

Undeniably, the organisational success of the Parent-Teacher Association in a secondary school essentially depends on a positive and sincere approach to pupil-advancement in learning. It is high time that every school takes a greater initiative for this end in view. Today's pupils will become parents tomorrow. Do we not really expect better roles of parent-teacher associations of today?

6

THE SCHOOL CUMULATIVE RECORD CARD

Prospects and Priorities

Education today necessitates all-embracing awareness. It may introduce many plans and programmes, projects and policies but what is more important is to see whether all these are actually pin-pointed, error-free and result-oriented. For all these purposes, the school cumulative Record Card is not only important but also mandatory.

Admittedly, what is normally found in the name of the school cumulative Record Card is a sheet of paper that very often than not exhibits bare informations with no specific strategies for spelling out furtherance of pupil-activity or pupil-progress. Moreover, pupil-teacher-parent relationships are hardly nourished by such a recordless record. In fact, when no accord for better pupil-advancement is established by a record, it should either be eliminated or improved. Unfortunately, the academic world is unusually embarrassed by a certain sense of passivity and inaction that has stood in the way of taking newer approaches and broadening worthier avenues of pupil creativity and critical thinking. A re-thinking on better approaches to the school cumulative Record Card is, therefore, very necessary.

Catchment Areas :

With a view to introducing the school cumulative Record Card, the following need immediate attention:

(i) Analysis of the School plant in a synoptic manner.

(ii) Physical dimensions encompassing school, class, section, grade, session, roll no., sex, class teacher etc.

(iii) The Record of Pupil-health.
(iv) The Record related to philosophical, psychological and sociological aspects of pupil-advancement in education.
(v) Statistical interpretations of pupils' all-round progress.
(vi) Analytical descriptions of evaluational keys of the Record.
(vii) Pupil self-assessment Record: Analysis and Suggestions.
(viii) Parents' Assessment Record: Analysis and Suggestions.
(ix) Teachers' Assessment Record: Analysis and Suggestions.
(x) Post-Evaluational Turn-keys.

A MODEL

A model of the school Cumulative Record Card may be suggested:

The School Cumulative Record Card : A Suggestive Model

I. *The School Plant : A Short History.*

II. Name of the Pupil ....
Class...........Section............Roll No..................Phase/...........Class Teacher
Grade/............Room/..................Sex..............Semester................
Standard..............Cluster..............Session..............Part...............

III. *Record of Pupil-health*

Date of Birth...............Height...........Weight.............Vision...........
Parents' names ....
....
Any other information ....
....

IV. *Community informatics*

Location of home..................................
Name of the next-door neighbour...
profession..
Name(s) of companion (s)/ ....
peers/...
playmates...
Community-Participation by the pupil in...
....

How far is the community favourable/unfavourable
to pupil-academic progress.. ....
Reasons...
Suggestions for improvement, if any...

V. Pupils' Schoolastic Record:

Subject	F.M.	H.M.	M.O.	Grade	%	Position	Class-Teacher's note	Any other Remarks

Explanation of Abbreviations
F.M. Full Marks
H.M. Highest Mark
M.O. Marks obtained
Percentage of marks obtained.

Grade : A+ = 80% & above
A = 70% to 79%
B+ = 60% to 69%
B = 50% to 59%
C = 40% to 49%
D = Below 40%

VI. Analysis of Evaluational Keys

Improvement pattern (s)
Blockade Area (s)
Reason (s)
Suggestion(s)...............

VII. Pupils' Self-Assessment Record

(a) Scholastic Record:	Performances	
Language Group	Mother tongue %	Other languages %
	....	....
Science Group	....	
Humanities Group	....	
Technical Group	....	
Home Science Group	....	

Agriculture Group ....
Fine Arts Group ....

(b) Scholastic-allied Areas:	Success-Analysis	Analysis of Deficiencies, Disadvantages

Creative performance...
Critical performance...
Aesthetic performances.......................................
Co-curricular Activities performances.................

VIII. Parents' Assessment Record

* Scholastic Areas : suggestions........................
* Non-scholastic Areas: suggestions...........................
* (Separate sheets are to be supplied)

IX. Teachers' Assessment Record

Name of the teachers	Subjects	Remarks*
....	....	....
....	....	....
....	....	....

* (Separate sheets may be attached)

X. Post-Evaluational Turnkeys

Analysis of strategies to be launched:
Subject...
Date and time allotted...................................

It may be noted that the above model is suggestive but not exhaustive and alterations/additions may be made in accordance with pupil-progress.

It may also be noted that the school cumulative Record Card is always directed towards some ends in view and never an end in itself. It aims at a continual development of pupil-progress from diverse avenues of excellence.

If today's education demands an overhauling of the existing patterns of pupil-evaluation, the school Cumulative Record Card is undeniably a pointer to re-orient our evaluation schedules. The constraints related to pupil-excellence can be better and more scientifically arrested through a well administered School Cumulative Record Card. Why not appropriately introduce it at every secondary school in our country right now?

7

QUESTIONING IN SECONDARY SCHOOLS
Strategies for Organisation

It is often said that answers are ample and questions are rare. This is not only an apt criticism of life but even in imparting lessons on the part of a teacher or in learning a lesson by pupils. What is significantly revealed is that hardly questions satisfy the desirable avenues of enquiries and perfection. Consequently, the gaps thus allowed to be retained hinder a pupil from being equipped with more essential weapons of reasoning and probing deep into the demain of innovation and creativity. Moreover, teacher-pupil interaction verges towards the matter of fact, dull and drab ideas and informations that rarely contribute to critical and creative awareness. As Voltaire characteristically remarks : 'Judge a man by his questions rather than by his answers'.

In fact a study of the different questions set on various subjects by the Boards of Secondary Education in different States of India for the last ten years will prove the following pecularities:

- (i) The set pattern is not always graded and sequential.
- (ii) Random sampling, instead of being geared to desirable and satisfactory evaluation, has drastically betrayed evaluation of pupils' critical and creative endeavour.
- (iii) Room for suggestivity is severely caged and cornered.
- (iv) Real life situation is extra-ordinarily eliminated.
- (v) Synchronization of facts and figures, on the one hand, and supposition and hypotheses, on the other have often been surprisingly ignored.

With all these undeniable but not necessarily unavoidable, facts (lacunal), secondary education is, alas, a more or less mechanised stage of learning that rests hopelessly assured of doling out certificates for biased, aimless, parochial, incomplete performances ! As experiences stagger at us in the most bewildering manner of course, in some part of the country or other, pupils hardly find interest in attending classes or remain unusually passive at the time of learning inside the class rooms. Again the so-called examinations either conducted by the school authorities or by the Boards often turn out into a farce. Hooliganism runs riot, malpractice reigns supreme, pupils devoted to studies become a poor prey to melee of mockeries and the wails of askance rend the air with the dominant and all pervading cry : O Questions ! What, then is questioning?

It is :

(a) a form of a specific enquiry-direct or indirect-verbal or, at times, non-verbal,

(b) to find out, from the person asked, answers related to numerous behavioural patterns and variations

(c) to add further avenues of enquiries such as complex, innovative, critical and creative ones,

(d) to arouse self-askance in both the asker and the askee.

A good teacher, as we all know, was asked : "What is the key to your being so good a teacher"? "I continually toss the questions", was the reply, "upon my mind to find out better ones to be retossed and answered." Indeed, the art of questioning is not merely an art. It is an art of all arts and science of all sciences.

A study of the different types of questions might pave newer avenues of questioning in secondary education. The following areas should be scientifically, adequately, intelligently and appropriately covered at the time of questioning :

Questions related to different stages of teaching.

(1) Preparation
(2) Presentation
(3) Application

Needless to say, the weightage of questions to be asked in different areas depends upon the actual class-room situation ascertaining pupils' previous knowledge, considering their average age and studying the learning atmosphere favourable or unfavourable.

Characteristics of Good Questioning

What are the essential characterisitics of good questioning? How can we say that questions asked or set to be replied or answered are really worthwhile?

A good question will signify the following :

(i) It is relevant or relevance biased.
(ii) It is simple.
(iii) It averts answers of 'yes-no' pattern.
(iv) It is directed towards a definite, single answer.
(v) It is unambiguous.
(vi) It is appropriate.
(vii) It is graded and sequential.
(viii) It invites logic of argument.
(ix) It is specific.
(x) It is clear and categorical.
(xi) It is comparison-contrast oriented.
(xii) It is similarity-dissimilarity oriented.
(xiii) It is interesting and curiosity evoking.
(xiv) It points towards further avenues of learning.
(xv) It helps forming hypothesis.
(xvi) It helps in framing rules.
(xvii) It helps in checking different points of learning.
(xviii) It helps in probing through different graded information-items.
(xix) It helps summarisation/comprehension.
(xx) It widens critical approach and creative thinking.

A few 'Musts' in asking questions

(a) Pupil preparation-readiness.
(b) Total pupil-involvement.
(c) Repetition only when absolutely necessary.
(d) No explanation excepting exceptional circumstances.
(e) No fumbling.
(f) Avoid baffling questions.
(g) No trickery in language-patterns.
(h) Allow room for critical and creative thinking.
(i) Be conscious of time to be asked/answered by pupils.
(j) Allow room for questions to go ahead.

As questioning is, as referred to earlier, the science of all sciences and art of all arts, why not re-orient ourselves with better avenues of questioning so that our pupils in secondary schools might be saved from receiving 'sub-standard' education, for practically no fault from their end?

8

ORGANISING MICRO-TEACHING FOR IMPROVEMENT OF TEACHING IN SECONDARY SCHOOLS

Teaching, as we all know, is a difficult task and teaching the young boys and girls particularly in secondary schools is more difficult because the teacher has to bridge the gap between experience and expression and/or between understanding and translating into reality. What is more interesting is that teaching that specially necessiates proper planning and trying out the most appropriate and judicious avenues of finding out the inner potentialities of an individual pupil, often lacks the verve and pulsating echo of adventure - the adventure of leading the young learner to know the unknown and to assimilate.the knowledge achieved in the throb of varieties and variations. Hence, micro-teaching.

Micro-teaching aims at qualitative improvement in teaching. With this aim in view, it has both the approaches— the convergent and the divergent ones— so that the area of knowledge and appreciation can be most thoroughly and elaborately appropriate. As the arena of micro-teaching, is initially arrested from specific points of end view, and a particular skill is analysed and re-analysed through its components, the knowledge thus spelt out within a limited period — say, five minutes only is evaluated and re-evaluated in terms of discussion and re-discussion in a controlled group.

A continual shuffling of plan-teach-dicussion re-plan re-teach re-discussion enables a teacher to locate the real avenue of desirable teaching behaviour to be manifested in a real class-room situation. With all consequences arrived at through simulated courses of teaching,the real platform is not merely forewarned but also sufficiently forearmed and the joy of teaching is never lost sight of by the teacher. Again, when dealing with numerous teaching points what hampers the progress of teaching is the absence of integration of teaching skills-a must for the teacher to offer teaching intstructions and to receive the best possible answers from pupils. Apart form the fact that the integrating approach to teaching is achieved in course of micro-teaching, the differentiating approach can be most successfully taken up by micro-reaching simply because a keen and cautious look at qualitative improvement in teaching embraces the unique potentialities of an invididual from all possible points of view. The gadgets applied and the other teaching aids executed in micro-teaching might apparently mean an overdose of simplification or mechanisation or, again, a willing complication of teaching procedures but the fact is that, with every trying-out, complexities and ambiguities with regard to micro-teaching techniques can easily be wiped out.

While a micro-teacher in course of his simulated teaching condition takes only five students each reperesenting the dull, the average, the intelligent, the shy and the mischievious types of students respectively and the number of teaching skills is only one in a period of five minutes only, the practice made in this very controlled condition can hardly escape strenuous and worthwhile orientation that is in future to be geared to the real situation of teaching.

Otherwise, no teaching can be of any use to channelize our pupils to proper teaching atmoshpere and, as a consequence, to learning. In tabular forms, the setting of an ideal class of micro-teaching for improvement of teaching can be analysed in the following way :

TABLE – I : Micro-Tecaching Setting

Class-VII	Total number of students-5		
Time 5 minutes	..	..	Micro-teachers-1
Session-Teach/	..	..	time-keepers-1
Re-Teach	..	..	Observers-1
Teaching aids	..	..	Recorders-1
Represented	..	..	Interpretors-1
	..	..	Guides-1
	..	..	Teaching skills-1
	..	..	Components of teaching-skills to be exercised for each and every component.

TABLE–II : Micro-teacher (MT) Micro-students (MS)

(1) IMS	(2) AVMS	(3) SMS	(4) MMS	(5) DMS

IMS	Intelligent	Micro-Student
AVMS.......	Average	,, ,,
SMS	Shy	,, ,,
MMS.......	Mischievious	,, ,,
DMS	Dull	,, ,,

A crisis-cross of questions and answers along with repetition, re-direction and re-phrasing of components of a particular skill will not only awaken a sense of curiosity for learning but will also enable the micro-teacher to arrive at desirable conclusions on teaching techniques. The following table (Table-III) shows a probable turn-out for cross-avenues in questioning through micro-teaching:

TABLE – III : Cross-avenues in questioning through micro-teaching

Step I	MT	(A) SMS (B) SMS (Repetition)
Step II	MT	AVMS (Rediraction)
Step III	MT	AVMS SMS
Step IV	MT	MMS (Re-direction)
Step V	MT	MMS (Repitition) (After receiving correct response)
Step VI	MT	SMS AVMS DMS MMS IMS (Rep. + Red)

A re-orientation of all the programmes of micro-teaching to be lauched in secondary schools for improvement of teaching will certainly pave path to newer directions for attainment of a real platform in the sphere of value-orientation in eduaction. While a careful look at qualitative improvement in teaching will enrich every teaching programme of activities, a certain switch over from traditional and formal programmes of imparting instructions to psychological and scientific and at the same time functional and human resource-oriented ones will ultimately lead to desirable advancement of learning. In this connection, it might be asserted that micro-teaching for imrovement of teaching in secondary schools is a means to an end, and never and end in itself. Moreover, it is not a substitute but supplement for better teaching. Obviously, it is a surer step to march ahead for educational reconstruction and improvement of standards in teaching. And so, why not launch micro-teaching vigorously?

9

ORGANISING OPERATIONAL STRATEGIES FOR VALUE ORIENTATION IN SCHOOL EDUCATION

Search for an all-embracing Value System

Education to-day, it is admitted by all, is undergoing terrible stress and strain. Finer values and softer sensibilities of life are replaced by dull and drab artificialities and a certain sense of passive attitudes and abstractions towards every aspect of life. Toady's pupils in schools, colleges and universities greatly suffer form a gradual erosion of values. With seek, hurry and divided aims, a pupil, right at the secondary stage of school education, becomes a victim to value disillusion because he/she sees all around an atmoshpere of utter incoherence and lack of work-ethics. And so, whatever education he/she receives, lacks exposures and continual refinement of his inner self.

The Report of the Education Commission (1964-66) refers to the importance of introducing education for social, moral and spiritual values in the school curriculum:

> A serious defect in the school curriculum is the absence of provision for education in social, moral and spiritual values. In the life of the majority of Indians, religion is a great motivating force and is intimately bound up with the formation of character and the inculcation of ethical values. A national system of education that is related to the life, needs and aspirations of the people cannot afford to ignore this purposeful force. We rcommend, therefore, that conscious and organized attempts be made for imparting education

in social, moral and spiritual values with the help, wherever possible, of the ethical teachings of great religions.

—*Report of the Education Commission (1964-66)* Ministry of Education, Government of India, 1966. Chapter VIII. p 206.

The role of the teacher is to enable pupils to inculcate the essential values of life by means of participation in different co-curricular activities. The strategy in each item of value to be exercised must be an indirect one and must also be based on the principle of conformity with individual differences in the diverse spheres of life. This is the only way to avert and arrest rampant`crisis of character' specially among young learners in schools. As the above mentioned Report suggests,

We attach great importance to the role of indirect inluence in building up good character. The school atmosphere, the personality and behaviour of the teachers, the facilities provided in the school will have a large say in developing a sense of values. We would like to emphasize that the consciousness of values must permeate the whole curriclum and the programme activities in the school.

It is not only the teachers in charge of moral instruction who are responsible for building character. Every teacher, whatever be the subject he teaches, must ensure that, in the teaching of his particular subject and in his dealings with his pupils, fundamental values such as integrity and social responsibility are brought out. The teacher need not, we can even say that he should not, try to draw out the underlying moral all the time: but if he has given some thought to the values underlying the scope of his subject and his work as a teacher, they will imperceptibly pass into his teaching and make an impact on the minds of his students. Moreover, a sense of purpose should inspire all school activities and must be reflected in the life, tone and atmosphere of the school. The school assembly, the curricular and co-curricular activities, the celebration of religious festivals of all religions, work-experience, team games and sports, subject clubs, social service programmes—all these can help in inculcating the values of cooperation and mutual regard, honesty and integrity, discipline and social responsibility. These values have a special significance in Indian society today, when young men and women are passing through a crisis of character.

— *Ibid.*

Undoubtedly, this sorrowful picture of value-erosion makes us aware of the truth exposed through the following words as set forth in *Challenge of Education : A Policy Perspective* :

> "Thoughtful people in all walks of life are greatly disturbed by a progressive erosion of values and the resultant pollution of public life. The fact that this crisis of values is as pervasive in schools colleges and universities amongst teachers as well as students as in other walks of life is seen as a highly dangerous development. It is, therefore, being urged that the process of education should be reoriented and young people should be made to realise that exploitation, insecurity and violence cannot be contained nor can an organised society be sustained without adhering to and enforcing some norms of social, political and economic behaviour learning from past experience; it is expected that a coherent and an operationally viable value system would be inculcated through educational processes, based a upon rationality and a scientific and moral approach to life."
>
> (*Values and Modernity* 1:24, p.10)

That the objectives of introducing education for value-orientation in schools should be considered in the light of the above perspectives can hardly be over-estimated. Who denies that a pupil in a secondary school is ever buoyant with pulsating social, moral, intellectual and ethical values? Who, again, averts that it is the ardent responsibility of teachers to launch effective programmes for manifestation of pupil-refinements and pupil-sensibilities towards right directions in secondary schools?

Two-fold Avenues

The operational strategies for value-orientation in secondary schools might be steered from two-fold avenues:

(a) Introspective and, (b) Apparent.

The Introspective Avenues might be built upon the following that await exposure, exercise and development among pupils:

(i) Team spirit/unity, (ii) Respect for other activities, (iii) Sense of Responsibility towards oneself and towards others, (iv) Creative Appreciation and critical consciousness, (v) Sympathy, (vi) Loyalty, (vii) Frankness and simplicity, (viii) Modesty, (ix) Tolerance, (x) Punctuality.

For (b) the operational strategies might be geared to exposure and exercise of the following :— (i) Good Manners, (ii) Hospitality, (iii) Sincerity, (iv) Co-operation, (v) Service towards others, (vi) Dignity of labour.

It might be pointed out that the two-fold avenues explained from the points of view of operational strategies for value-orientation are inter-dependent and mutually exclusive. Even then the finer points of departure amongst them might be exercised from individual viewpoints. As a matter of fact, the more one delves deep into one's own sensibilities, the more is the possibility of an aura of new dimensions that beckon newer horizons of value - orientation.

Strategic Modules

For effective value-orientation in school education, the following Strategic Modules might be considered :

Strategic Module 'A' : Analytical Perspectives

1. Identification → of Areas	2. Functional Avenues →	3. Term → ↙↘ Short term / Long term	4. Analysis of Evaluational Approach ↓
	7. Remarks ←	6. Remedial ← Measures Suggested	5. Diagnostic Measures Adopted

Strategic Module 'B' Pupil's Notebook

1. Total number of Social activities organised by the school	6. Operational Advantages	
2. Total number of social activities attended/performed	7. Operational Limitations	11. Assignments for the future
3. Specifications of Activities	8. Any other remark in connexion with operational Advantage/ Limitations	12. Analysis of Assistance riceived from (i) Teachers (ii) Parents/ Guardians
4. Skill (s) exercised		

5. Operational Aids used

10 Period(s) covered

(iii) Class-mates
(iv) Others

13. Type of Assignment
14. Remarks

Strategic Model 'C' : Orientation of Teachers

1. Programme of Activities Identified
2. Total Hours Involved
3. Total Number of Pupils Involved
4. Analysis of Work-Design
5. Report of the Orientation-Programme
6. Post-Evaluational Dimensions

Towards The Depth of Truth, Beauty and Goodness

From a study of the above modules as operational strategies for value-orientation in school education, it might be noted that every sincere endeavour towards unfolding the inner world of every pupil might open out newer avenues of understanding and appreciating truth, beauty and goodness. The real challenge of education is to march ahead : *Charaiveti.* The heartland of everyone interested in education must be inspired and stimulated to that end-in-view. Let every pupil share and enjoy values that nursle the finer visions of mankind. Let him/her be allowed to explore out of his/her own spontaneous endeavour the heartland of humanity anew and afresh to usher forth a new era of emerging values. Do we really channelize our school education towards that direction with all care and caution?

10

ACCELERATING CREATIVE AND CRITICAL APPRECIATION

Waiting for the 'inward eye'

Education *sans* creative and critical appreciation is simply meaningless. In the words of Rabindra Nath Tagore, it is equivalent to parrot's learning that deals with dead, matter-of-fact, stuffy, bookish facts of life. It has nothing to do with human sensibilities. The finer and the softer visions of life are lost in the melees of abstractions and mechanical drudgeries of learning. But then, with all these shortcomings notwithstanding, education today is suffering from a definite sense of inadequacy in sheer utilitarianism. When education is primarily concerned with careless doling out dull passports for the formidable future to learn for the sake of learning alone, with meagre exposure to the 'inward eye' as one might recall Wordsworth, it endlessly enjoys unaccounted holidays in the arena of self-enrichment and self-askance.

At the backdrop of the constraints consequent to the above maladies of education, it is high time to revamp education towards the right direction that would usher forth a new area of creative and critical appreciation. Admittedly, re-designing education to this end-in-view necessitates a re-thinking of the strategies of introducing manifold approaches to unfold and enkindle pupil-creativity and pupil-appreciation right from the secondary schools. In this connection, it might not be inappropriate to refer to the fact that in most of the states of our country, language-learning is mostly concerned with the cognitive level of pupil-understanding and remains more or less passive to enkindle pupils' creative, critical and aesthetic sensibilities. Is automation fast gobbling up the finer emotional responses of everyone to be utilitarian in every approach whatsoever? Perhaps the ambiguous aim of learning a language-second, foreign, link, official or otherwise, gained and capitalized, in order to have a working knowledge is still more interested in chaff or husk than in the grain of appreciation through creative and emotional exposures. This is not all. The transfer of learning from one discipline to the other through an approach to critical and creative appreciation becomes an alien affair.

That education is being continually commercialized needs a look back and a look afresh in the arena of individual emancipation in better exposing oneself in course of creative exercise and critical thinking. In secondary schools, this sort of qualitative change in education is not only desirable but also mandatory.

Objectives

Keeping in view the above perspectives of education the following objectives might be considered for accelerating pupils' creative and critical appreciation in secondary schools:

(i) To enable pupils to apply their critical and creative faculty of imagination and appreciation to every item of experience and study, whenever possible.

(ii) To stimulate pupils to enter deep into the vast domain of intrinsic and introspective matter of life, and associate themselves with the discovery of the newer world of creative and critical appreciation.

(iii) To encourage pupils to be practised in the comparative and contrastive study of numerous experiences and expressions as set forth or experimented upon by the author (s) of a particular theory or item, and to arrive at their own unparalleled point of conclusion.

(iv) To allow pupils to contribute their own models of perfection in creative and critical appreciation.

(v) To enable pupils to be inspired with widening their approach to creative and critical appreciation through a study of real life situation under the guidance of a teacher who stimulates the avenues of awareness to manifold visions of life.

Strategies

As strategies to the above objectives, a secondary school might ponder over the following for pupils of different stages:

A. *Junior stage* : Classes V and VI

Work schedule :

(i) Study of lessons that provokes creative imagination.

(ii) Pointing out easy imagery-patterns.

(iii) Identification of simple imageries.

(iv) Telling/Expressing similar simple imagery-patterns.

(v) Summing up in general through creative appreciation.

(vi) Study of beautiful objects of Nature.

(vii) Enjoying dramas, stories, poems and so on.

(viii) Practices in appreciation to VI and VII.

B. Middle stage : Classes VII and VIII.

Work schedule: In addition to the above as stated in 'A', the following might be considered:

(i) Stimulation to the aesthetic appeal of Nature.

(ii) An inquisitive appeal to the varied facts of life and experiences.

(iii) Application of critical thinking and creative appreciation to any incident or affair of life.

(iv) Practice in comparative study.

(v) Study of easy symbols and rhetorical expressions, and applications of a pupil's own creative and critical faculty of imagination and appreciation.

C. High stage: Classes IX to X,

Work schedule: In addition to 'A' & 'B' as stated above, the following might be covered:

(i) Individual identification. Analysis and appreciation to creative and critical experiences.

(ii) Group Appreciation Programmes.

(iii) Analysis of rhetorical and prosodic nuances with special reference to individual creative and critical sensibilities.

(iv) Symbolic variabilities and imagery-analysis.

(v) Assimilative and creative role of pupils assigned to a certain pattern of imagery embracing individual creative appreciation.

Introducing Exercise of creative and critical Thinking through Writing and appreciating Instant Poems in Secondary schools

Model:

Stage: Middle : Classes : VII & VIII

Work schedule : Composition of instant poems on the following:

	:	Birds, Aeroplanes, Trains, Flowers
Topic	:	Birds
Type	:	A four-line poem
Rhyme-Pattern	:	a b a b
Keys: General	:	Birds fly with flapping wings The blue sky Joyfully sings.
Autobiographical	:	I an a bird I flap my wings, The song is heard The blue sky sings.
Expositional strategy	:	Small with the topics on one side in each of them are placed on a table with written side downward. Each pupil is allowed to take up one card and directed to compose and instant poem of four lines. If the topic is not upto the pupil's liking, a second chance is given to draw another card and is directed to say an instant poem of his own on the topic. Reinforcement and feed-back may be given as occasion demands. But a forewarning should be there lest the unique imagery-patterns of a pupil might be destroyed through interference.
Evaluational strategy	:	Evaluation should be made strictly on the basis of pupil-endeavour and pupil performance. Self-evaluational dimension should be made wide open. Post evaluational suggestions should be precise, pin-pointed and constructive. At Santiniketan, the above is a very common programme for efflorescene of pupils' creative and critical appreciation.

Summing Up

Accelerating creative and critical appreciation in secondary schools is long overdue. On the threshold of a new era of education for qualitative change, pupil-excellence in exposures necessitates emancipation of individuality that, again, calls for deeper and saner involvements of subjectivity. Undoubtedly, to negotiate these objectives, teachers themselves must be creative and critical in their approach to teaching. The prime question is: Are we, teachers really so?

11

ORGANISING AESTHETIC EDUCATION

The Breakthrough

Education throughout the world is undergoing a rapid change. In India, too, whatever experimentations are going on in the arena of education are primarily oriented to exploring and exposing the desirable human behaviour. Apart from the fact that a developing country necessitates explosions in education, this does not necessarily indicate that we should bid good-bye to all human values and finer sensibilities and softer emotions of life. Rather is it an inevitable factor that the search of an individual for manifestation of his inner potentialities through education is the need of the hour.

Already, with the introduction of the Report of the Kothari Commission (1964-66), it has been increasingly felt that to immediately and satisfactorily negotiate (challenge) all round bankruptcies in education, a breakthrough in our educational systems in the secondary stage particularly—stage so delicate and vulnerable—is, beyond doubt, a must. And, with a view to achieving the above objective in view, the introduction of aesthetic education for emancipation of creative and critical appreciation is one of the major steps that can hardly be denied for qualitative education.

With all spree for quantitative education married to utilitarianism, educationists have seriously felt the erosion of sensibilities in human life. Young boys and girls in secondary schools consider their Alma Maters not more than thriving factories doling out certificates, diplomas and degrees endearing unemployment and desolation throughout their future life. Moreover, such an education alien from allowance of pupil-spontaneity and creativity coupled with a thrilling urge for critical appreciation for what is true, good and beautiful cannot but embrace hopelessness and drudgery—a fact we have, indeed, realised not merely from theories or hypotheses but from down-to-earth realities of life.

Education, to be really dynamic, and, therefore, living must open out vistas of humanized activities that have a soothing and lasting effect of sympathy, fellow-feeling and mutual understanding. *Sans* love is *sans* education that paves path to modesty rich in the ardent desire to know within oneself the hidden resources of humanism. Hence, the efflorescence of aesthetics in human life.

Aesthetic Education in Secondary Schools : Objectives

To inculcate the spirit of aesthetics for emancipation of creative and critical appreciation among pupils in secondary schools, the following points might be considered:

(i) to enable pupils to foster the spirit of creative spontaneity and critical awareness through comparing and contrasting different patterns of thought and exposing the inner feelings logically and systematically.

(ii) to enable pupils to analyse manifold patterns of imageries in the unique way through exercise of individual critical and creative potentialities so that further avenues of aesthetics might see the light of the day.

(iii) to enable pupils to identify, imitate and/or criticise the pattern of thought that they come across through individual/group study, discussion and so on and to evolve the individualistic pattern of aesthetic appeal that might be registered as an outcome, though not in legion but a little (but not altogether insignificant) humble contribution to aesthetic sensibilities developed through endless endeavour.

(iv) to enable pupils to be equipped with all round aesthetic sensibilities to enter into the wonderland of the True, the Good and the Beautiful.

(v) to accentuate the spirit of softer visions of life as, for example, nursing the distressed, helping children, the old and the infirm, looking after national properties, maintaining civic sense, forming habits of cleanliness, sanitation, truthfulness and the like.

(vi) to maintain and adhere to strict principles of discipline, particularly the inner one that alone contributes a lot to a pupil's control in human behaviour that, again, contributes a lot to his control of emotional and social disintegration.

(vii) to be cautious on the part of a teacher to expose himself/herself before his/her pupil and to enable his/her pupil to have his/her guidelines for manifestation of creative and critical consciousness.

(viii) to enable the pupils to emulate virtues inherent in every aesthetic appeal intrinsically spelt out in theoretical and/or practical discussing activities.

(ix) to enable each pupil to maintain a personal note book or diary to record events or items he/she comes across significant for emancipation of his/her creative and critical appreciation.

(x) to introduce the system of maintenance of the pupil's Cumulative Record Card to record, analyse and evaluate exercise of the pupil's creative and critical talent and to suggest further avenues of betterment.

(xi) to introduce the system of self-assessment card for evaluation of pupils' creative and critical efflorescence in the arena of aesthetic activities by themselves.

Organisation of Aesthetic Education in Secondary Schools : A Suggested Model for Emancipation of Creative and Critical Appreciation

A Few Forethoughts

The following forethoughts on the model suggested might direct towards desirable efflorescence of aesthetics through individual pupil's creative and critical appreciation:

(i) Proper identification of AIA and AOA is sometimes very difficult but for better emancipation of creative and critical appreciation the purpose of identification can hardly be ignored.

(ii) The four areas of AIA, namely Aa Sim An, AaOD and AaV are so delicate and intrinsic that each area necessitates further pinpointed analysis for better identification and exposition thereafter.

(iii) AaOD, while compartmentalised in ID and OD, is the area of difference leading to individualistic approaches to aesthetic development. But, then, IDCF and IDHL arising out of ID and ODMAIPC, ODIPCSL and ODIPCEL split up from OD, each of which contributing to newer avenues of aesthetic appeal, allows an individual both from personal and social standpoints of excellence, and a synchronisation of all would lead to exercise and manifestation of aesthetics through creative and critical appreciation.

(iv) That aesthetic education in secondary schools is better organised might have its acid test by ODMAIPC through further analysis of its three areas viz., GACVOE, AEIPC and SIPCA and they are so inter-related that if GACVOE, for instance, remains absent, the other areas viz. AEIPC and SIPCA might not see the light of reality.

(v) AaIV and AaEV, the two components of AaV are undeniable factors for aesthetic appreciation. For further identification and analysis, while AaIV and AaEV embrace IVr GIGL IVctt IGL and EVICC EVGA respectively, greater, care should be taken to individual pupil's development of IVrGIGL and IVttIGL which are better caught than taught.

AIA: Aesthetic activities having inward appeal to senses and imaginations.

AOA: Aesthetic activities having outward appeal to senses and imaginations.

AaSimAN: Aesthetic activities contributing to succinct imagery-analysis.

AaCCS: Aesthetic activities contributing to comparative studies

AaOD: Aesthetic activities related to observance of discipline

AaV: Aesthetic activities related to values.

AaIV: Aesthetic activities oriented to internal values.

AaEV: Aesthetic activities oriented to external values.

AEIPC : Amiable exposition of an individual pupil to the clientele.

EVICCc : External values related to individual creative and critical consciousness.

EVGA: External values related to Group Appreciation

GACVOE : Generous Allowance of clientele's views and opinions to be expressed.

IVrCIGL: Internal Values readily contributing to individual and group life.

IVCttIGL: Internal values contributing form time to time to individual and group life.

ID: Inner Discipline

IDCF: Inner discipline contributing to character formation

Organisation of Aesthetic Education in Secondary Schools: A suggested Model for Emancipation of Creative and Critical Appreciation.

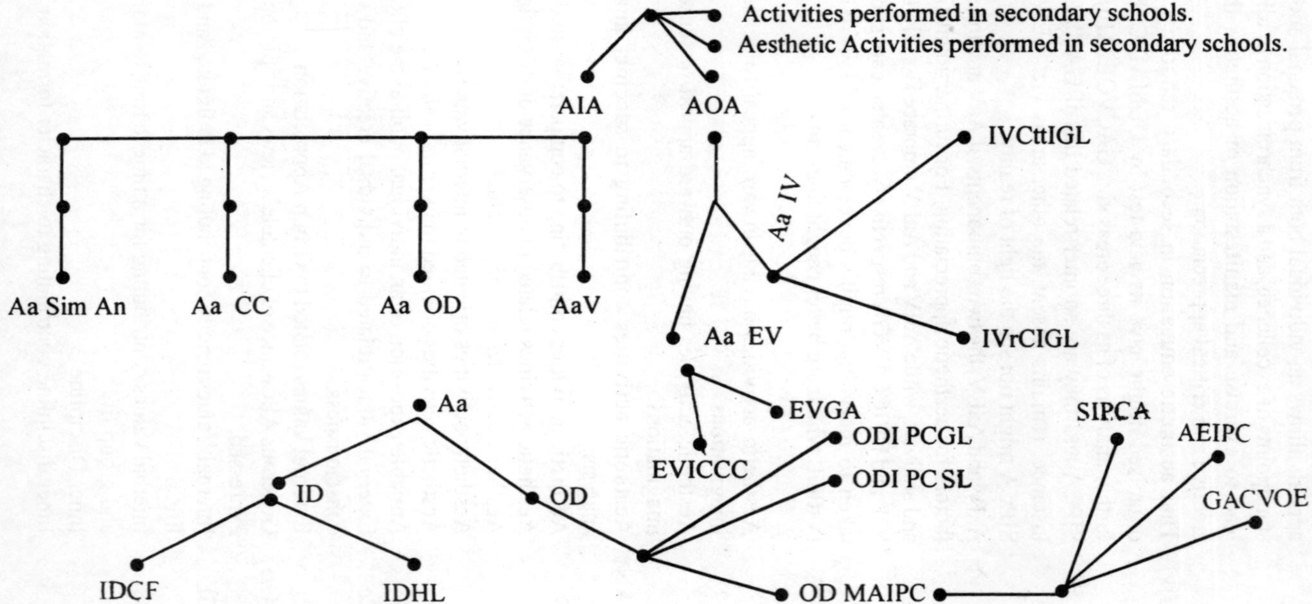

IDHL: Inner discipline regulating habits of life.
OD Outer Discipline
ODIPCGL : Outer discipline related to an individual pupil's contribution to group life.
ODIPCSL: Outer discipline associated with individual pupil's contribution to social life.
ODMAIPC : Outer discipline regulating manners and approaches related to inter-personal communication
SIPCA : Synchronisation of inter-personal communication approaches.

Summing Up

Our march for a truly effective education specially in Secondary Schools needs a re-oriented approach to aesthetic education so long ignored in the plea that it is nothing but exhibitionism in the name of educational reconstruction or a romantic vein that evaporates out of chivalrous attitudes towards man and life. To usher in young minds the spirit of aesthetics is one genuine way of preparation for nobler visions of life to be translated into reality. The spurt of creative and critical appreciation that pulsates a pupil inside/outside the classroom necessitates an opening through revelations of aesthetic sensibilities. Who knows the awakening of softer visions of life that haunt him/her like a passion would beckon a world of oneness—a World of the Great Family of Mankind.

12

TEACHING POETRY IN SECONDARY SCHOOLS

Organisational Avenues

Poetry as well all know, is the innermost language of mankind. It is a language which is, in the words of Samuel Taylor Coleridge, arranged in 'best words, best thoughts and best expressions'. Perhaps the essence of human personality which is itself poetry, indicates the culture-consciousness of human civilization, an expression rather devalued and throttled in the mechanics of a macabre era.

The fact is: a look at the present system of education in our country particularly at the secondary stage-not to speak of the primary one that miserably fails to impart and initiate the spirit of poetry right from the beginning of a pupil's entrance into the wonderful world of knowledge, wisdom and erudition-does not properly provide room for the emergence and exercise of his finer sensibilities and softer emotions of life. Instead, learning a language with a view to attaining a working knowledge for bare livelihood or at best for mere communication of artificial, dull, drab, down-to-earth drudgery takes the upper hand in the teaching of poetry. What a tragedy!

A study of the different syllabi of secondary school education boards all over India will point to the fact that in language-learning the role of pupils' creative and critical thinking has not been appropriately identified and spelt out, and the avenues for newer strategies have not been clearly and innovatively geared. As a matter of fact, whatever education is imparted through our teaching of poetry at this stage fights shy of embracing the world of pupil imagination and creative and critical sensibilities–queer, incomparable, invaluable, unique, boundless, delicate and multi–dimensional.

Moreover, development of moral, social, emotional, intellectual, cultural, ethical and aesthetic sensibilities can hardly ignore the surest possible strategies to be adopted in the teaching of poetry, and poetry alone, that continually prepares a young learner to modify his behavioural abnormalities or loopholes in the light of finer expressions and delicate sensibilities.

Psychologically, language and behavioural manifestations are so closely interlinked that a pupil's experiences in terms of a particular thought process play the intrinsic game of hide-and-seek amid development in different stages viz, those of incubation, illumination, assimilation and verification, each of which can and should, again, be analysed from temperamental and temporal view-points.

As pupils in secondary schools meet and experience the stage of adolescence, the above psychological factors in connection with language-teaching and behavioral manifestations can hardly be over emphasised. To take a single but prominent point of pupil-behaviour, chivalry, a sign of efflorescence of adolescence. It turns into sham romanticism which, through exercise of poetic sensibilities in creativity and critical thinking in restraint, might bring forth rich dividends in becoming a man of excellence in future. Again, hero-worship another module of romantic urge in adolescence, that lovingly wishes its marriage with distant reality beckoning him to the world of infinite wonders — dies down in the drought of teaching poetry where creative and critical imageries are nourished in the workshop appreciation of utilitarian perspective.

Consequently, absence of pupils' social development in the identification, assimilation and exercise of social sensibilities through poetry culminates in their passive and at times evasive attitude to social ills and disparities. A sense of disillusionment and a certain sense of social irresponsibilities which have more or less become a craze of modernity in the community find a happy breeding ground in the denigration of individual creative and critical potentiality. Whither humanity. The lost horizon of human consciousness is yet to usher forth the awakening of the spirit of oneness amongst mankind—a spirit that can be silently manouvred through poetry for creative and critical enlightenment of individuality.

Objectives

Keeping in view the above points, the objectives of teaching poetry for efflorescence of creative and critical thinking in secondary schools can be spelt out in the following ways:

(i) to identify and analyse pupil-imageries contributing to the manifestation of creative and critical sensibilities.

(ii) to identify and analyse the conceptual mode of pupil-behaviour expressed in a lesson on poetry.

(iii) to identify and analyse how far pupil-imageries are enriched by ones experienced through and expressed in reaction through the teaching of a particular poem.

(iv) to identify and analyse how far a comparative approach to the teaching of poetry heightens and, at the same time, sustains the spirit of pupil's creativity and critical thinking.

(v) to identify and analyse how far teachers' own contributions to poetry fill up the pupils' creative and critical sensibilities.

Avenues

In order to make an effective approach to the teaching of poetry for creative and critical thinking in secondary schools, the following might be taken up as one of the strategies for experimentation in the actual classroom situation.

Identification and Analysis of Poetic Imageries

This can, again, be compartmentalised in three groups :

(a) Texture of Poetic Imageries
(b) Structure of Poetic Imageries
(c) Style of Poetic Imageries

The particular areas of each pupil's poetic imageries to be identified and analysed in accordance with the above three groups may be arranged in the following table as a record and further study of pupil-performance:

RECORD CARD

Name of the pupil :........................Session: Teach/Re-Teach.........................

Class:.......... Section :........... Roll No. .... Age: .... Sex :..........

Span of the period : .... Orientation/Reorientation Type:

Total Number of Ques- tions asked or presented	Total Number of ques- tions responded to by the pupil	Total Number of ques- tions failing to arrest pupil attention	Reason for (3)				
			A	B	C	D	E
1	2	3	4				
			Very Diffi- cult from Con- cep- tual point	Not adequate- ly ex- plained	Not Con- sistent- ly appro- ached	Not Rele- vant	Not clear simple easy to approach

5	Reason for (5)		6		
	A	B	C	D	E
Total Number of questions paving further avenues of curiosity	Supple- mented by the teacher's own con- tributions	Divergent areas of attention and interest	Related to pupil's self ex- pression to Creativity	A pointer to added avenue of Creativity	Rich in Suggesti- vity and in-depth expressions

A close look at the above table suggesting newer avenues of teaching poetry in secondary schools might throw a bolder challenge to so-called abstractions and ambiguities in poetic imageries often sandwitched in the protest of silence. Should we not allow our young learners to enter into the wonderland of poetry : to strive, to seek, to find and not to yield?

13

THE SCHOOL COMPLEX

Problems and Parameters of Organisation

The school complex is the outcome of the Report of the Education commission (1964-66). The Commission makes an intensive enquiry into the appalling differences in standards of education imparted in the secondary schools of our country where students suffer from inward and outward complexes. These complexes are revealed in the differences between the rich and the poor, the high and the low, the advantaged and the disadvantaged, the affluent and the starved student–communities in schools. Ironically, the quality in education aimed at is thrust forward in the face of all these trying situations where education turns out to be a mockery in relation to unfavourable social and school climate.

To bring about a really effective change in school education, it is undeniable that pupils must be emancipated from isolation and poverty in qualitative education. The essential reforms aimed at to negotiate this primary end in view as suggested by the Commission above may be referred to as follows:

— A common school system of public education should be evolved in place of the present system which divides the management of schools between a large number of agencies whose functioning is inadequately coordinated.

— A nation-wide programme of school improvement should be organised with three objectives : (a) to raise all schools at least to a minimum prescribed level; (b) to assist every school to rise to the highest level of which it is capable; and (c) during the next ten years, to raise at least ten per cent of the institutions to an optimum standard.

— The offices of the District Educational Officers should be strengthened and the existing techniques of supervision should be replaced by new methods which emphasize guidance, objective evaluation and provision of extension services.
— The State Institutes of Education should be strengthened.
— State Boards of School Education and State Evaluation Organizations should be established at the state level – accompanied by the creation of a corresponding machinery at the national level–to stimulate a continuous improvement in standards and to assess them periodically.
— The Central Government should develop a large programme in the centrally–sponsored sector to assist in the improvement of standards at the school stage.
— Report of the Education Commission, "School Education : Administration and Supervision", Ministry of Education, Government of India, 1966, Chapter X, p. 849.

An effective function of the school complex as envisaged by the Commission will yield the following :

(i) It will introduce 'better methods of evaluation' and regulation of promotion of pupils from one class or one level of school to the other.
(ii) provision of better facilities in equipment, library, laboratory, etc., for every school under the complex will be possible.
(iii) Utilization of service of teachers specialized in physical education or other teachers both in the normal school hours and beyond will be effective and fruitful.
(iv) provision of leave substitutes for teachers in schools under the complex will be effective.
(v) Innovative programmes on school education under the school complex can be elaborately chalked out, implemented and all teachers and pupils under the complex may be harmoniously involved.
(vi) In-service programmes for improvement in teaching can be launched in the scheme of school complex and teachers may be benefited in qualitative teaching.
(vii) Arrangements for periodic meetings of teachers to discuss

latest issues in improvement of teaching and pupil-excellence in education may be made in course of seminars, symposia, conferences etc. under the auspices of the school complex.

(viii) Plans and programmes on introducing common text books, strategies for selection of pupils for different levels, orientation and improvement of standard of school text—books, ensuring better evaluation criteria and diverse other issues related to qualitative education for pupils may be effectively introduced in the school complex.

(ix) Teachers interested in innovative research work on the diverse dimensions of the school complex may be allowed to enjoy and exercise in abundance experiences encountered in visiting schools under the complex and exchanging opinions with teachers, administrators and others associated with school education.

(x) A national forum on the problems and perspectives of school complex may be convened in which teacher-educators particularly concerned with pre-primary, primary and secondary education exchange their views and opinions on smooth and effective functioning of the school complex.

Catchment Aeas

The catchment areas of the school complex may be tabled as follows:

TABLE : 'A'

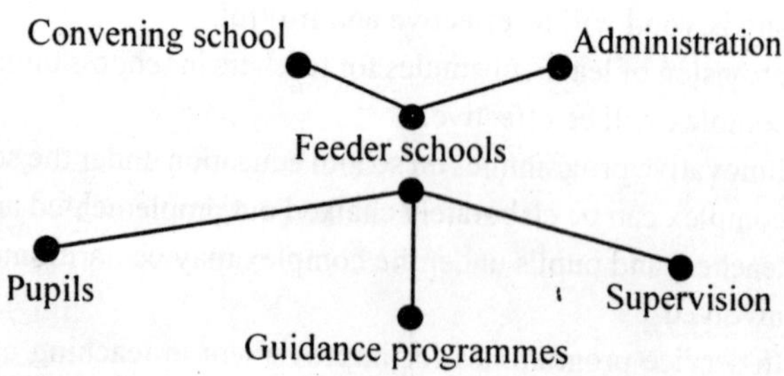

TABLE : 'B'

School Complex

Feeder Schools

Teachers	Teaching complexities and constraints
Administrators	Administrative complexities and constraints
Pupils	Constraints and complexities in learning
Parents/Guardians	Rapport complex and constraints
Other members of the community	Rapport complex and constraints

TABLE : 'C'

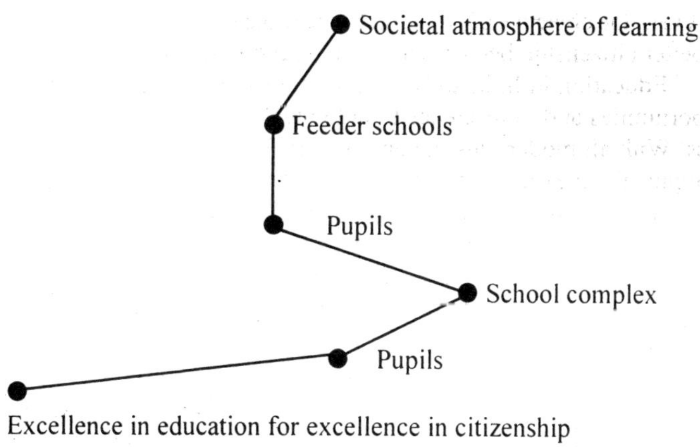

From a study of the catchment areas as identified in Tables 'A', 'B' and 'C' it is evident that the school complex has an arduous responsibility for better organisation and co-ordination of schools under its control. The convening school maintains relationship with the feeder schools under the school complex in a very careful and cautious manner. It has to look after pupil-progress in all directions on the one hand and maintain on the other a cordial relationship among all concerned specially in administration, supervision and organisation of guidance programmes. Needless to say, the complex primarily passes through an acid test of its organisational abilities and efficient endeavour in course of dealing with intricate matters of school administration, supervision and guidance under delicate and complex academic environment.

The chained relationship among teachers, administrators, pupils, parents and guardians and other members of the community awaits better negotiation of adverse circumstances where administrative complex and constraints affect healthy relationship between the feeder schools and the convening school. As a consequence, absence of adequate and healthy rapport between the teacher and the taught, the teacher and the parents/guardians or even between the teacher of the convening school and that of the feeder ones defeat the very purpose and significance of the school complex.

The school complex cannot but organise a societal atmosphere of learning which, alas, is badly lacking in the school climate at present. The pupils hardly care for social synchronization even in the crudest form in schools which miserably fail to cater to education for social harmony. If the school complex seriously adopts organisational strategies for implementing social activities specially designed and directed towards acceptance and acceleration of better social sensibilities among pupils at all levels, the objective of promoting excellence in education for excellence in better citizenship becomes assured in school organisation.

Education in India today stands at the cross-roads of affluence of opportunities and indifference to individual creative and critical awareness. With all modern instruments and appliances amply introduced for bringing about excellence in education, what is undeniable is that education suffers from being localized or centralized in vulnerable pockets at the invaluable cost of public exchequer. As a consequence, the difference between the rich and the poor, the high and the low, the rural and the urban, the privileged and the denied continues unabated. The so called cosmopolitanism — the forbidden fruit, as it were, of the garden of Eden in education — and the lure of urbanization take a firm grip over easy, rustic naturalness and simplicity in the desirable arena of modernity and progress in education. Exhibitionism and apeing of crudities and posh affluence of utilitarianism strongly stand in the way of natural and spontaneous understanding and appreciation of mutual endeavour in education that provides growth and development of a healthy body and mind of each learner.

In the backdrop of the above, the limitations in the present day system of school education specially with reference to school organisation may be identified and analysed as follows :

(i) Today's school education invites dissociation. The avenues of opportunities between the rural and the urban schools are poles apart.

(ii) While in many schools specially located in urban areas desirable educational opportunities are abundantly available, and good education, therefore, is imparted without any major constraints in educational instruments and appliances, libraries and laboratories and so on, pupils in rural schools are yet to be provided with minimum educational opportunities as above. Consequently, the latter are nursled with sub-standard education well-enough to prepare sub-standard citizens of future.

(iii) With private schools growing like mushrooms in the melee of sub-standard and opportunistic educational climate, education now is a commodity to be 'bought' and is hardly aimed at to be 'caught'. Ironically, almost everyone is interested not in education in the real sense of advancement of learning but in being affluent in manipulating education for consumerism and exhibitionism. Consequently, education today is brought down to the level of a rapidly thriving industry where cultivation of learning is transformed into trickeries in earning.

(iv) With education imparted in different schools under diverse socio-economic conditions there is hardly any sharing of mutual life and experiences. This invites undemocratic atmosphere in the altar of education and also breeds happily the thriving seeds of disintegration. Moreover, the finer sensibilities and the softer visions of life are blurred in a jaundiced atmosphere.

(v) While honesty, devotion to truth, simplicity and all other moral and ethical values are greatly desirable for every pupil learning in schools, these are more often vitiated with appalling differences in scopes for manifestation of pupil-personality. Moreover, absence of or abundance in initial spurt for every learner determines how he would manifest himself through exercise of individuality.

(vi) With variations of opportunities in different schools for different types of students, the entire curriculum is oriented towards that end in view. As a consequence, this affects pupils' approach to learning and living, too.

(vii) It is undeniable that schools with better educational instruments and appliances provide pupils with room for better educational experimentations with the help of laboratories, while those bereft of all these, turn education into mere daily drudgeries.

A careful study on the observations of the Education Commission (1964-66) reveals the following facts with regard to the schools complex:

(a) Schools are open to all learners irrespective of caste, creed, complexion, sex, social position, religion and so on.
(b) Good education for every learner — poor or rich, advantaged or disadvantaged — must be provided.
(c) No tuition fees for learners should be imposed in schools.
(d) Qualitative school education should replace time- worn, mechanical, drab and passive education.
(e) Elimination of expensive schools nourishing the wills and aspirations of the affluent and negotiating the neglected needs and aspirations of average parents and guardians for their hapless learners are to be carefully considered in implementing the aims and objectives of the schools complex.

Organisational Parameters

The Education Commission (1964-66) has rightly suggested for a two-tier complex in its organisational aims and objectives, which would embrace the entire pupil-community in school education.

A further spell-out of these tiers has of late become imperative as pupil-teacher rapport necessitates a closer tie. This may be tabled as follows:

TABLE: 'D'

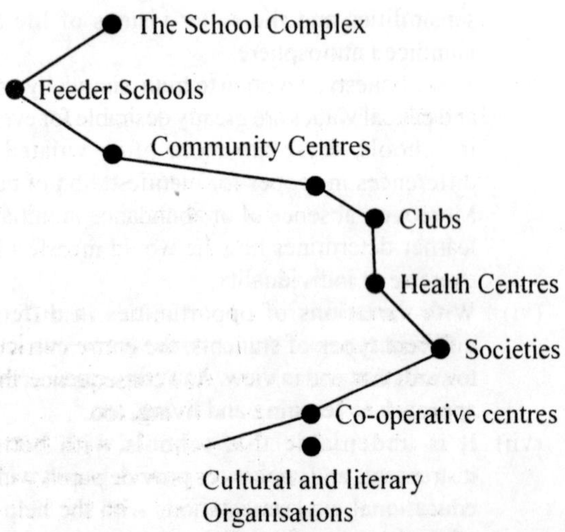

From a study of the above, it may be suggested that for qualitative school education, the school complex should be so organised and disseminated as to familiarize learners with the organisations around them. As a matter of fact, the school complex, for better organisation, must come nearer to the clubs, health centres, societies, co-operative centres, cultural and literacy organisations in particular. Otherwise the entire school complex will remain isolated from these diverse organisations that amply contribute to every pupil's development of personality.

The feeder schools in a school complex and the community centres undeniably necessitate a closer tie than mere apparently mutual relationship when occasion demands. There are certain glaring problems in a community viz. health and hygiene, illiteracy and apathy where feeder schools should come forward with newer programmes for community development. They should organize exhibitions on different items of community development and allround consciousness of mass education.

Admittedly, the school complex should incorporate a few specific organizational activities to boost feeder schools and the community which include:

(i) Enrichment of the feeder school library.

(ii) Arrangement for holding group discussions, seminars, workshops etc, where pupils and teachers of feeder schools actively participate along with the members of the community.

(iii) Invitations to noted community workers and experienced educationists to highlight latest trends and tendencies in community development.

(iv) Introducing essay contests, poster display, role playing, survey work among pupils of feeder schools to eliminate narrow interests and foster the true spirit of community consciousness.

As every school is a miniature community the school complex serves as the most vital factor of development of community centres. Our schools at present fail to identify this fact. It is high time, our organisational avenues in school development and school education accept the challenges of constraints towards fulfilment of objectives for dynamic and living education. Do we believe and rise up to the occasion?

14

CLASSIFICATION OF PUPILS

Organisational Avenues

Education is essentially an instrument of change. It allows the learner to undergo behavioural changes that lead to development of personality in all directions. In schools the very educational instructions that are imparted through daily activities are to a large extent geared to academic excellence. This, however, does not always ensure a healthy and all round development of pupil-personality. Very often in routinized bookish education, the points of individual similarities and differences are either ignored or weakly dealt with for fullness of growth and development. As a consequence, every learner is walled in the dark city of ignorance in some vital matters of interrelationship as well as of uniqueness of personality.

A desirable and scientific classification of pupils always necessitates an appropriate comprehension of the ideas and purposes of schooling of children at the very outset. Why do parents send their children in schools? The answer lies in negotiating their two crucial problems *viz.*, the problem of socialization and the problem of control. The problem of socialization is one of channelizing the child towards accepting and practising rules and habits of group living, group activities, group understanding, analysing, appreciating and evaluating all forms of experiences towards which the child is exposed. Side by side with these, the child should be allowed to exercise individual traits of personality which contribute a lot to qualitative socialization so sadly missing in our endeavour at better organisation of education specially in secondary schools.

The problem of control of children by parents or guardians is actually a biased one with vested interests. Modern parents with their full-time involvement in outdoor activities hardly take up the challenge of bringing about desirable changes in pupil-personality amongst their own wards. In most cases, there is a shirking of responsibility well substantiated by the theories and trends of specialization even in child education. That parents or guardians cannot control their wards and, therefore, seek refuge in schools for better education for individualization and socialization are the source points of pupil indiscipline that makes the problem of organisation of children in schools more acute. Today's schools start with a constraint of indiscipline and unsocial pupil-clienteles who have already been immuned with obsessions from home atmosphere and home surroundings. Any good organisational programme of activities should, therefore, be based on a thorough investigation and survey of home atmosphere and parental attitudes towards their own pupil-entrants in schools.

Classification of pupils demands better organizations in schools because the fundamental objective of education, as it should be, is to individualize instruction and socialize the child. In a classroom situation in practice, pupils have, indeed, some points of similarities in the areas of knowledge, understanding, skills, interest, attitude, aptitude and appreciation. This does not necessarily ensure the fact that they are all alike or should be treated in the same manner so far as imparting instruction is concerned. Rather is it desirable that the teacher should also identify points of individual differences amongst pupils along with those of similarities so that better individualization and worthier socialization through appropriate teaching strategies are possible. Any successful endeavour at school organization should, therefore, explore diverse avenues of efflorescence of pupil-individuality and at the same time formulate and work out programmes of synchronization between individualization and socialization. Indeed, for effective organisation of teaching in schools, classification of pupils serves as a means to an end and never an end in itself.

Classification of Pupils for individualized Instruction

Organisational Dimensions

Bearing in mind individual differences among pupils in schools in knowledge, understanding, interest, skill, attitude, aptitude, appreciation and so on, organisation of school specifically for maintenance and development of better learning-teaching atmosphere is not only desirable but also obligatory. The organisational dimensions form this end in view may be stated as follows:—

(a) Since every learner is typically unique in his approach to experience and learning, individualized instruction greatly contributes to enrichment of uniqueness in pupil-personality.

(b) The pupil-teacher ratio in learning-teaching is 1:1 and as such both the teacher and the pupil enjoy the most favourable atmosphere of advancement of learning.

(c) Since there is no problem of joy and freedom in learning-teaching atmosphere, both the learner and the teacher enjoy an ideal atmosphere of learning and teaching, and hardly any organisational constraint of critical nature stands in the way of pursuit of learning and teaching.

(d) There is hardly any problem of indiscipline and truancy in individualized instruction and learning situation as both the learner and the teacher are widely exposed.

(e) The pupil feels a new wave of enthusiasm and aspiration within himself in innovative study and research as he can unhesitatingly submit his innovative designs and intricate matters in research activities to his teacher. This, of course, works in an embrionic form in a school learner but it is the teacher who well organizes in close association with his pupil newer avenues of negotiating manifold problems in the most efficient, reliable, purposeful, economic and individual manner.

(f) Pupil-appreciation to learning is greatly enriched in individualized instruction. As the teacher becomes well aware of the learning potentiality of his clientele, he organizes renewed or changed atmosphere of learning for better efflorescence of individuality through qualitative teaching designs.

(g) Better socialization of pupils in schools becomes a reality through better individualization. Every pupil in a well organised atmosphere of individualized instruction is in a sounder position to know and experiment with emergent social norms and needs and becomes deeply involved in diverse social problems.

Keeping in mind the above dimensions of individualized instruction, the teacher in association with the academic and the administrative personnels of the school can organise and implement programmes of qualitative education for each individual learner as follows:

(i) Introducing a *Diary of Pupil Progress* to maintain a record of the latest trends and tendencies of pupil-progress in learning. individualization, and socialization.

(ii) Providing every pupil with opportunities for undergoing diagnostic and other tests as and when necessary.

(ii) Stimulating the innovative spirit of every leaner by allowing him to actively participate in different programmes like science clubs, history clubs, seminars on language and literature, preparing models, charts, maps etc.

(iv) Holding exhibitions, fairs, debates and discussions on numerous issues where every individual learner contributes to the best of his abilities.

The *Diary of Pupil-Progress* is very significant so far as organisation of individualized instruction is concerned. The parameters of this Diary may be analysed in terms of the following table:

TABLE – 'A': The Diary of Pupil-Progress: Physical Dimensions

Name of the pupil...Class/ Grade:
Section ....Roll No. .... Year.................

First quarter (January-March)
Second quarter (April-June)
Third quarter (July-September)
Last quarter (October-December)

Name of the Teacher.................................

TABLE – 'B': The Diary of Pupil-Progress. Behavioural Perspectives.

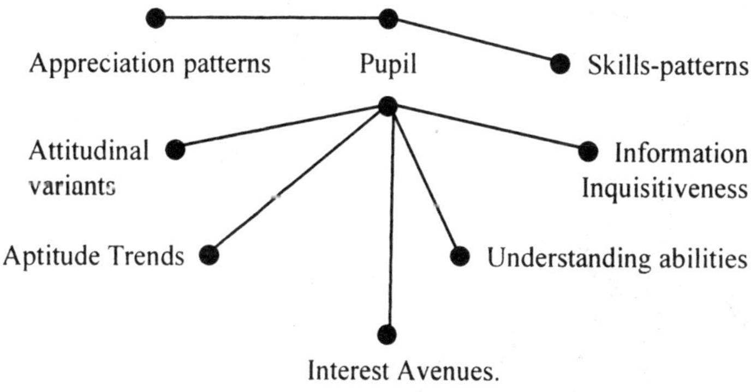

TABLE –'C': The Diary of Pupil-Progress: Organisational Parameters

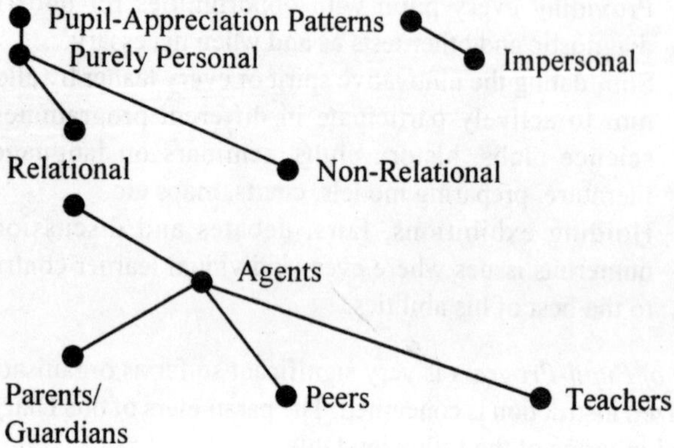

Attitudinal Variants in Pupil-Appreciation

(i) Relations manifested in terms of expressions verbal and non-verbal
(ii) Attitude towards social norms
(iii) Attitude towards peer-suggestions
(iv) Attitude towards parental pointers or directions
(v) Attitude towards the suggestive/advisory opinions of teachers.

The Diary of Pupil-Progress should substantially contribute to better organisation of school education. With regard to attitudinal variants as spelt out above, wider scope for exposure of pupil-reactions–both verbal and non-verbal— should be provided. The social norms should be so elucidated by the teacher as to encourage his pupil to ventilate his own contribution in the form of criticism constructive as well as dynamic and operative. The teacher should also organise cultural and social programmes where the individual learner welcomes peer suggestions and the advisory or suggestive opinions of the teachers to enrich individual excellence in thought-patterns and appreciation and at the same time nursles a healthy and growing opinion of man and society. The teacher also gears the aptitude trends of every pupil towards fullness of growth and personality.

As in individualized instruction the interest avenues of pupils are more clearly exposed than in group instruction, it is the duty of the teacher to identify the manifold avenues of interest components of his pupil and orient his teaching strategies to boost the positive points of nurturing those components. If necessary, he familiarizes his pupil with newer avenues of interest by involving himself closely to the interest patterns of his pupil. As a consequence, individualized instruction so imparted becomes very fruitful and appropriate.

Perhaps the most characteristic point of school education is organisation of a pupil's understanding abilities from the very beginning of imparting individualized instruction. For this, the teacher explores the diverse avenues of diagnosing his pupil's information inquisitiveness and involvement in selecting or rejecting skill-patterns. His primary role is to organise ample provisions for exercise of his pupil's creative and critical excellence. A few remarkable plus or minus points of his pupil's endeavour towards this direction noted in the *Diary of Pupil-Progress* from time to time makes individualized instruction a potent force to dynamic school organisation.

The above does not minimize the importance of organising school education for imparting group instruction. Rather is it variable for any progressive thinking on organisation of school education to mobilize the spirit of socialization in a better and more convenient way by means of group instruction. What, then, are the positive points for better classification of pupils as aimed at through organization of group instruction? A study of the following elucidates the answer better:

(a) The primary objective of classification of pupils is to organise and to be assured of better teaching learning situation. A successful organisation of teaching and learning is well-ensured in group instruction as it fully encompasses motivation in group of pupils.

(b) The burden of the teacher is lessened by pupils sharing and criticizing their own views and opinions among themselves in group discussions and group participation. Moreover, the spirit of co-operation which is really very difficult to be instilled in a pupil under individualized instruction becomes an easily comprehensible matter when pupils undergo exercises in education through group instruction.

(c) As organisation of education by group instruction is a time-saving affair, the proficiency of the teacher as an organizer often becomes no serious and vulnerable affair in case of group instruction. The pitfalls of teaching and learning are sometimes covered by pupils through group discussions.

Classification of pupils for group teaching necessitates organisation of pupils in a homogeneous or a heterogeneous manner. As both homogenous and heterogeneous groups have psychological bearings, classification of pupils under these two groupings demands a forewarning of the following for better organisation of school education:

(i) In organising instruction for homogeneous groups of pupils care should be taken to eliminate any type of complex both in case of learners and that of teachers.

(ii) The school itsalf must not be allowed to exhibit complex or complcency which unduly disturbs efficient organisation.

(iii) In organising education for pupils in a heterogenous group all tendencies towards parasitical, mechanical, routinized, passive and dull teaching and learning should be well arrested. The motivational force expressed in a class-teaching atmosphere should be regulated in terms of efflorescence of individual excellence and discipline.

(iv) Any successful programme for organisation of education on the basis of classification of pupils lanunched either homogeneously or heterogeneously requires at the outset a thorough analysis of the norms of classification and as such the school should cater to this end in view of classification of pupils.

Organisation of education in schools in accordance with classification is, indeed, a very delicate and complex affair. Right from the Dalton Plan by Helen Parkhurst and the Winnetka Plan by Carleton Washburne down to programmed learning, micro and mini teaching etc. the fundamental point of interest is how far organisation of education is justified to classification of pupils and how far the school climate or the classroom climate is favourable to pupils for excellence in individuality and sociability.

With the Dalton Plan aiming at organization, laboratory work and group discussion and devoting to pursuit of learning in an exhaustive and elaborate manner, the whole process of organisation of education becomes highly expensive and time consuming besides unusually intricate and complex. Again, with organisation of education according to the Winnetka Plan which spells out school education in terms of common essentials and group activities, pupils fail to have a specific entry into the individual subject to be studied at length and at the same time suffer from proneness to truancy in the plea of group activities.

Admittedly, the very purpose of classification of pupils for better organisation of school education is defeated in an atmosphere of undesirable objectives to be achieved for individualization and socialization of pupils. Any attempts at hurried or aimless classification will lead to deficiencies in organising better school education.

Classification for the sake of classification alone is of little worth. It is undeniable that classification enhances pupil-progress in education but that should be well supported by the motto in organisation of education: Individualize instruction but socialize the child. If the teachers are well stuck to this principle of organisation in classification of learners, learning becomes joyous, living, pulsating, meaningful and thrilling. Do we follow this principle?

15

PLANNING SCHOOL PROGRAMMES

The Planning of programmes in education in secondary schools has of late undergone revolutionary changes. The schools today are more aware of their resources and constraints, care more for objective-based activities and devote more to positive evaluational performances. The relationship between the primary school and the high school and that of the high school and the higher secondary school have become more cordial and interdependent. Consequently, better planning of school programmes has been a natural tendency in any endeavour at better organisation of schools.

Why planning school programmes? What are the organisational know-whys in planning school programmes? A careful enquiry into these problems and queries of planning school programmes opens out newer perspectives of school organisation as follows:

(a) A genuine and effective organisation of school programmes almost entirely depends on the teachers who best know how to plan comprehensive school programmes and how to work out these programmes effectively and efficiently. It is the teacher who from his day to day experiences in class-room teaching locates the deficiencies and points out advancement in pupil-learning and suggests effective programmes of school planning. Unfortunately, his suggestions are most often ignored and he is rather forced to organise and implement hypothetical programmes already chalked out by experts in education from ivory towers. Moreover, there is hardly any rapport between the administrative personnels and the teacher in planning effective school programmes and, as a result, the teacher and the administrative personnels continually suffer from delicate and strained complex.

Again, besides mere undergoing in-service training for once only throughout the whole period of service to be officially stamped as 'trained', a really sincere and devoted teacher pines away in the four walls of a classroom repeating and re-organising the same plans of imparting instruction. Even his non-verbal expressions, if video-taped by a secret arrangement, are exactly the same year after year. This certainly indicates a morbid end-spurt in his motivational activities for better organisation of instruction. This is further aggravated by lack of opportunities for professional enrichment and for innovative experimentations. A major cause for today's passivity and alienation from school planning and organisation by teachers is that they do really consider themselves 'not-wanted' persons in school education.

(b) As today's school education in our country is almost entirely dependent on grant in aid received from the government and is also blessed with other financial receipt, there is a certain deficiency in organisational alertness and involvement on the part of school administration and supervision. This also leads to proneness towards a parasitical approach to growth and development. This again also acts as a hindrance to a practical approach to economy and better utilization of resources. While there is a certain tendency towards shirking of mutual responsibilities for better organisation of school education and administration among teachers on the plea of paucity of required number of instructional employees, pupils lose the lesson of learning how to utilize time and limited resources available from their schools. A sense of love for the institution which grows out of better organisation of school education is thus neglected in day to day teaching learning programmes in most unplanned institutions.

(c) In an unplanned organisation of programmes of activities in schools, education becomes a concern for none but showmanship for everyone. Lack of organisation in such a situation in school education means lack of initial programmes of activities which act as prerequisites to better school education. These initial programmes of activities may be spelt out as follows:

(i) *Survey Work*

This ensures a proper school climate for better organisation of education. A careful survey work scrupulously investigates into the purposes and possibilities of organisation of a school in a certain area, place or a community centre and it also looks into every detail of need-based future programme of activities covering the entire areas.

(ii) *Planning of School Programmes*

Any organisational approach to school education necessitates appropriate, objective-oriented, scientific and fool-proof planning of school programmes. As such, planning of school programmes includes suggestions of teachers, students, administrative personnels of the school and also appreciates community suggestions received from time to time for better school education. A good planning of school programmes also endorses and highlights suggestions from eminent persons in every walk of life. It also encapsulates the experiences of the past and the future possibilities of better outcome of school organisation.

(iii) *Execution of School Programmes*

The Planning of school programmes once finalized awaits immediate implementation. A thorough check-up of the plan before execution is, therefore, undeniable. At the time of execution of school programmes strict observance of discipline and punctuality is also necessary. Otherwise, the plan of activities in the school may not be completely worked out.

(iv) *Evaluation of School Programmes*

Evaluation of school programmes is one of the most essential factors of school organisation, supervision and administration. How to be ensured of better evaluation of school programmes of activities? The following table shows the different parameters of evaluation:

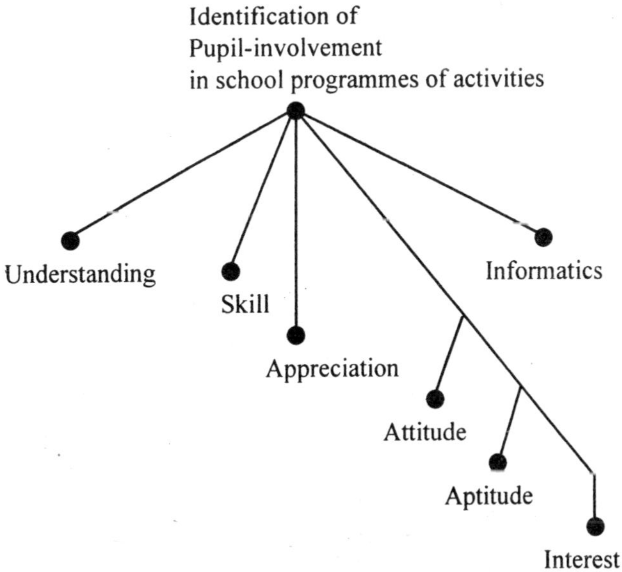

While identification of pupil-involvement in understanding and informatics in school programmes of activities are to a great extent dependent on a continual and careful evaluation of pupil-participation, it is the duty of the teacher to provide ample opportunities of self organisation and self-activity for every pupil. If necessary, the teacher may directly involve himself in school programmes and set a model for this end in view. This organisational approach to school programmes of activities may also be fruitfully extended to other areas of pupil-involvement e.g., appreciation, attitude, skill, aptitude and interest.

(v) Post-evaluational approach to school planning

All evaluational activities in connection with organisation of school planning require re-identification of plus points as well as the minus ones for encouragement and elimination respectively. Hence, a post-evaluational approach to every school planning. The specific components of post-evaluation should be carefully analysed in terms of pupil-acceptance and pupil-appreciation. As such, as post-evaluational activities in relation to organisation of school planning should be planned in accordance with the future needs and prospects for better school education.

Planning School Programmes: Catchment Areas of Organisation

Identification and organisation of planning school programmes have of late been raised to the level of superior attention and interest in school education. The following catchment areas of organisation, therefore, deserve appropriate attention:

(i) *School-Community Relationship*
Planning school programmes like visit to community centres, participation in community functions and festivals, arrangement of talks, lectures, seminars on items of school-community development and invitation to eminent community leaders come under the preview of organising effective school-community relationship.

(ii) *National Integration and Global Harmony*
Education is always an incomparable instrument of change from a man to 'men'. School education should, therefore, plan different programmes on accelerating national cohesion and global harmony and organise them from time to time. The pupils may also be encouraged to organise programmes on National Solidarity Day, U.N. Day, Children's Day etc. to exercise the spirit of national and global consciousness.

(iii) *Planning School Programmes for Improvement of Curriculum*
Organisation as such consists of programmes like discussions on how to improve the reading habit of pupils, how to ensure pupils with better use of the school library and laboratory, the school playground and the gymnasium, if any, and how to bring about an effective change in the system of internal examination. A planned school programme on any of the items above necessitates a concerted endeavour in organisation by all associated with school education. The school may organise programmes on improvement of text-books, teaching aids etc., which play a very significant role in the education of the child. Moreover, discussions on the above pave newer avenues of improvement of the school curriculum. The teacher also finds a genuine urge for involving himself in all these programmes for curriculum development because his views and opinions are adored and endeared.

(iv) *Planning School Programmes for Improvement of School Discipline*

This is a very important area of organisation of school education. The school may organise dramatic functions and discussions highlighting the importance of discipline and punctuality. Even the truant and the indisciplined pupils may be involved in role playing, actively participating in different school programmes on discipline and punctuality and evaluating their own involvement form time to time. Rigid discipline is thus relegated to the background and free discipline facilitates satisfactory pupil-progress in learning and behavioural designs.

(v) *Planning School Programmes for Efficient Organisation of Co-Curricular Activities*

Planned School Programmes on co-curricular activities of pupils contribute a lot to effective school education. Contrary to the concept that co-curricular activities are apathetic to regular course of curricular activities, there is a growing tendency now among teachers and everyone associated with the teaching of the child to vigorously synchronize subject with activity, since they believe that education is primarily a psychological affair that harmonizes intelligence with work. To channelize pupils to utilize their leisure hours by means of organising and involving them in different co-curricular activities like participating in school assemblies, science clubs, hobby clubs, *Sahitya Sabhas* etc. makes education more living and dynamic, thrilling and pulsating, than doling out dry instructions to them engaged in the four walls of the careless class-rooms.

Planning School Programmes: Organisational Personnels

A conjoint and communicated endeavour of all the organisational personnels in planning school programmes is not only desirable but also mandatory. An interchange of ideas and experiments among them in planning school programmes makes education more functional, regulated and fruitful. The whole body works in chained relationship, which can be analysed in the following table:

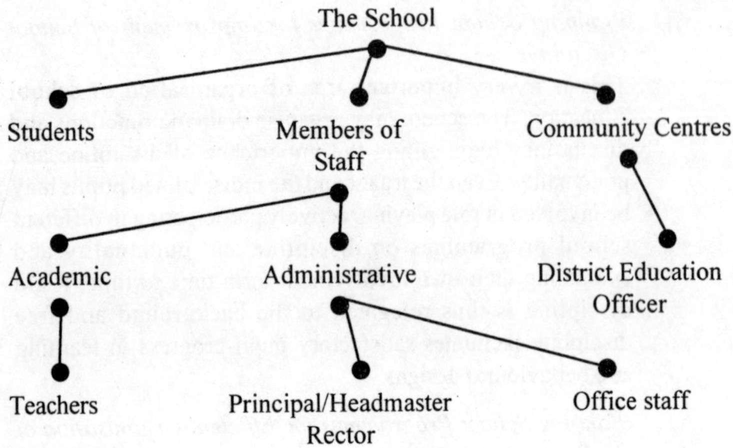

Organisation of healthy relationship among all associated with school education is an important parameter of school planning. As a matter of fact, modern theories and principles of organisation with regard to school planning and school administration are essentially geared to a more comprehensive approach to utilization of resources and man-power in the forms of expertise and economy. Celebrated organisations in our country like the National Institute of Education for Planning and Administration (NIEPA) and the National Council of Educational Research and Training (NCERT) are devoted to the purpose of effective school planning, school organisation and school administration.

Check-List for Organising Planned School Programmes

The following check-list may be considered for better organisation of planned school programmes

(i) Whether the planned school programmes are need-based.

(ii) Whether the planned school programmes incorporate the following components as and when necessary:

  (a) Flexibility
  (b) Changeability
  (c) Variability
  (d) Comparative viability

(iii) Whether teachers pupils, parents and others directly or indirectly involved in the planning of school programmes are well motivated through organisation of school activities.

(iv) Whether the planned school programmes are well spelt out in objectives, pin-pointed, free from any sort of ambiguity and fool proof.

(v) Whether the planned school programmes effectively contribute to all round development of the school.

The above check-list for organising planned school programmes is not exhaustive but suggestive and so in organising such programmes local and community needs should also be worthily considered as and when occasion demands. In fact, successful planning of school programmes is always related to organisational opportunities and constraints assessed in terms of local facilities and priorities. Often it so happens that in organising a planned school programme of activities, certain items of importance are left unattended while apparently insignificant ones are given major importance in work-schedules. This type of organisational flexibility invited and duly attended to in planned school programmes often brings forth remarkable and surprising dividends in qualitative education.

Planning Year's Work

Planning the year's work of a school has recently been given added importance in school organisation as it holds out the primary acid test of organising abilities. Admittedly, no school today dares work in an indisciplined and haphazard manner. The arduous responsibilities of planning the year's work of a school in systematic and regulated manner for smooth and effective organisation of school activities may be discussed as follows:

Preliminary Activities Prior to Opening the School

The work-schedule may be prepared on the basis of the composition of a Committee represented by

(i) The Principal
(ii) The Teacher representative
(iii) The student representative
(iv) A representative from the school governing body
(v) A representative from the local community
(vii) A representative from the District School Board, preferably the District Education Officer.

The above Committee would look into the preliminary arrangements for opening the school and discharge their duties as follows:—

Inspect the school campus including the school building, library, laboratory, playground, auditorium, hostels and staff quarters.

— Check the essential arrangements of services in sanitation, water supply, electricity etc.

— Look into the matters related to pupil-conveyance and information services.

— Arrange for *School Work Bulletin* which includes the following items:

(i) Teacher's Assignments
* Classwise/Gradewise
* Sectionwise
* Groupwise

(ii) Information to
* Parents/Guardians
* Pupil
* Hostel Superintendent
* School Librarian
* School Office: Administration
* Local Community Director
* District Education Officer

(iii) Preliminary arrangement for holding classes for
* New session with new entrants.
* Out-going students

(iv) Allocation of duties to
* School Office assistants
* School security and beautification services personnels

The *School Work Bulletin* also provides information with regard to the members of new entrants and transfer cases along with programme schedules of visit by eminent persons in different walks of life to the institution. It also spells out in detail the additional curricular and co-curricular assignments by teachers and others associated directly or indirectly with such activities.

Any successful organisation of the year's work of a school cannot but negotiate the problems of opening the school. Planning the year's work of a school, therefore, depends on the efficiency in tackling the following problems:

*How to restore normalcy in the school climate?
*How to arrange classes to be held regularly?
*How to plan the activities of the school for the first week?
*How to negotiate the rush of new admission and transfer?
*How to arrange staff meeting?
*How to involve parents/Guardians and others with the preliminary activities of the school?

Arrangements for framing a tentative time-table to avert lack of imparting instructions to pupils and indiscipline may be made in co-operation with teachers in charge of framing the school time-table. Prior to this, teachers may be requested to submit their suggestions for an effective tentative school time-table. When such a time-table is prepared, allocation of periods/classes should be well intimated to every teacher. A copy of such a tentative time-table should be properly displayed in the school well ahead, and parents/guardians will be informed about all policies and guidelines with regard to the following:

* Book-list
*Admission: Rules and Regulations
*Transfer: Rules and Regulations
*Course of study: Selection Procedures

Organisation of work in the first week is an acid test in planning year's work of a school. The tentative time-table for the first week, when introduced, determines the organising abilities of all concerned with the teaching and administration of pupils. It clearly reflects the total picture of the school to be aimed at by means of planning year's work.

The work in the first month of school is full of diverse responsibilities from organisational points of view. The school calendar already prepared after a thorough discussion among members of the staff awaits organisation for execution. Meanwhile, the plan of work submitted by teachers individually should be organised. Other areas of importance in organisation include guidance service for pupils, holding different class-tests and delivering assignments and homework to pupils, arranging supervisory programmes for teaching the gifted as well as the backward children and finalising dates for discussion on different matters of education in the Board of Studies.

A holiday list and a list of total working day of the school should be carefully and cautiously prepared and a copy of each of these lists should be delivered to every student in the very first month of the school session.

Needless to say, such lists facilitate pupils to be sincere and disciplined in every work curricular or co-curricular.

Programme of Activities Throughout the year

Planning school programmes of activities has its end in view in smooth organisation throughout the year. Here, too, good organisation depends on good distribution of work among all concerned in the well-being of the institution.

A well-coordinated programme of activities already chalked out should be effectively executed keeping an eye to all the principles and procedures. If necessary, minor addition and alteration of the programme of activities may be allowed for the sake of better organisation and supervision. The guidance programmes for individual and group pupil progress should be well checked before implementation and if necessary, consultation with experts form outside agencies to avert probable shortcomings should be made in advance.

Second, for desirable co-ordination in the area of organisation specially with reference to school administration the following administrative centres/organisations may be contacted as and when necessary:

* The local body/community
* The District School Board.
* The Board of Secondary Education
* The School Managing Committee
* Any other organisation related to the school.

Third, prior to school organising external co-ordination, organisation of internal cohesion of activities forms an integral part of planning school programmes and success thereof. Such co-ordination encompasses organisation of closer relationship between the student and the teacher, the teacher and the headmaster, the teacher and the parents, the student and the headmaster and so on. An efficient, organised and co-ordinated programme of activities in school education will always cater to the development of favourable atmosphere of learning in the school and pupil-personality. Moreover, the school, if so well organised in course of planned activities, would certainly draw the appreciative attention of the local community, and, as such, community participation for better organisation of the different work schedules of the school should become natural and spontaneous.

A good organisation of activities planned for a school is only a means to an end but never an end in itself. It must have the quality of giving proper direction to furtherance of qualitative excellence in school organisation and administration. The parameters of the direction may be identified as follows:

* Directing the gifted children towards better exercise of their potentiality and excellence.
* Directing the slow learners to undergo specific programmes of activities to eliminate deficiencies in learning.
* Directing the learner to effectively and efficiently utilize the school library and the school laboratory.
* Directing the learner to vigorously participate in the diverse programmes of the co-curricular activities of the school.
* Directing the learner to regularly and sincerely participate in games and sports and physical exercises.
* Directing the teacher to enrich professional efficiency by participating orientation programmes on different subjects, workshops, seminars, symposia and so on. The teacher may also be further directed to undergo training in teaching and increase his academic qualification through higher study.
* Directing different programmes of activities in the forms of meetings, conferences etc. to promote closer relationship between the school and the community.

Programme of Activities in connection with closing the School Year

Closing the school year necessitates organisation of the following activities:

* Conveying parents/guardians the progress or the deficiencies of pupils.
* Promotion of Pupils.
* The School Annual Report.
* Necessary Announcements.

To convey parents/guardians about the progress or deficiencies of pupils is to primarily be assured of all informations in connection with the curricular and co-curricular activities of the school in which the pupils have participated and assess in terms of their involvement. This assessment is to be made in accordance with fool proof measurement of pupil-participation and pupil achievement. There should not be any personal liking or disliking in terms of pupil-assessment of their performances and so all evaluation made by teachers should be carefully and cautionusly checked prior to conveying parents or guardians of pupils.

The promotion of pupils should also be objectively made and pupil performances of activities in school at all directions should be seriously taken into account. The behavioural aspects of pupils and particularly those related to morality, aesthetics, discipline and punctuality are also to be fairly and pin-pointedly evaluated.

The School Annual Report is not a mere conglomeration of details of problems mostly financial or otherwise normally read out and informed by the headmaster or his representative on the day of the prize-giving ceremony of the school but a real document that holds out the diverse avenues of school development and school activity. The essential components of the School Annual Report refer to organisation of the following items:

(i) A synopsis of pupil-attendance
(ii) A summary of pupil-enrolment
(iii) The school financial report
(iv) The salient problems with regard to
  * Class-rooms
  * Play-ground
  * Library
  * Laboratory
  * Sanitation
  * Drinking Water
  * Conveyance
  * Hostel accommodation
  * Security

(v) Curricular Activities comprising holding internal assessments scholarships, awards etc. Guidance and Supervision Programmes
(vi) Co-curricular activities
(vii) Educational tours and excursions
(viii) Social service
(ix) Individual pupil's outstanding performances
(x) Report of school games and sports
(xi) Report of school functions and festivals.
(xii) Highlights of Recommendations for the next year.
(xiii) Report of the receipts and expenditures

(xiv) Report of the community-participation of the school
(xv) Report of the innovative activities and other proficiency of the teachers.
(xvi) Future Prospects and Guidelines.

Admittedly, the School Annual Report acts like a mirror to reflect, as it were, the organisational role of the school for effective education and development of pupil-personality. Moreover, it acts like a magic wand to locate intricate deficiencies in teaching-learning programmes of activities often organised in a hurried manner.

A Special Bulletin at the time of closing the school year highlighting the following in a planned way would certainly indicate organisational clarity and precision:

* The schedule of the annual examination
* The schedule of the duties allocated to teachers for setting question papers, examining answer-scripts, submitting marksheets, completing progress reports, holding admission tests for new entrants for the next year, preparing routines for different classes for the next year, and suggestions for better teaching learning climate.
* A resume of the system of evaluation.

Planning school programmes is planning for better organisation of schools. It is a continual and strenuous endeavour but there is certainly a joyous and thrilling outcome in organisation of programmes. As such, planning of school programmes always beckons us to launch an adventure in organisation. Do we respond?

16

ORGANISING THE SCHOOL TIME-TABLE

The school time-table contributes a lot to the smooth and efficient functioning of the school. It enables disciplined organisation, administration, supervision and guidance of the school and directs all associated with the organisation of the school towards fullness of growth and personality of pupils.

What is a school time-table? From the philosophical point of view in education one can define it from diverse dimensions. Among some characteristic definitions of the school time-table from this point of view as above, the following may be identified and analysed:

(i) The school time-table is a portrait of the school in facts and figures in skeleton. Apparently abstract with numerous abbreviations applied in framing a school time-table, it holds out a true picture of the school to undertake and execute organisational activities in a planned manner free from all ambiguities and constraints.

(ii) The school time-table is, as it were, a magic wand to activate the whole institution in a regular and disciplined way. Through its magic touch, the total activities of the school are promptly and judiciously organised and nothing remains unattended to the dissatisfaction and disappointment of the teacher and the taught in particular.

(iii) The school time-table is a spark plug of the school. Whenever it is effectively introduced and organised, the whole school is switched on to thrilling and lively activities. As a matter of fact, it acts like a guide and stimulates everyone with directions planned and set forth in a well co-ordinated manner.

(iv) The school time-table is the second clock of the school. True to its metaphorical meaning, the teacher and the learner in particular are always warned against abuse of time through the different programmes of activities to carried out and completed in due time and it acts as a continual reminder of the duties and the responsibilities of both the learner and the teacher.

(v) The school time-table is a mirror of school activities. Just as a mirror reflects the image of any person or objects, it also reflects the different programmes of activities to be organised and performed in a disciplined way. It holds up the image of a school to be in future from what it was in the yore and what it is at present.

(vi) The school time-table is a disseminator of the philosophy of a school. It holds up the ideas and ideals in symbols and essentially awaits organisation and supervision with utmost sincerity and devotion. An apparent look at the school time-table instantly allows any visitor to visualize how the school functions during school hours on every working day.

One can go on adding and elucidating more philosophical definitions of the school time-table as above. All these prove the point that the school time-table is an invaluable instrument in school organisation.

Leaving aside all these philosophical interpretations as above, let us consider a few concrete and specific definition of the school time-table :

(i) The school time-table is a distinct and analytic map of the daily activities of the school. A look at the time-table designed as such clearly shows the total distribution of assignments for instructional employees at a scheduled period of time in a certain section of a class for pupils. The subject to be studied is also mentioned and sometimes the topic to be discussed is also announced. As a systematic chart of the entire school programme it helps a great deal to complete the entire course of studies in a well-directed and disciplined way.

(ii) The school time-table is a definite pointer to well coordinated and systematic activities to be performed all the year round in a school. It leaves no room for any incompleteness or ambiguity in pointing out the schedule of activities— curricular or co-curricular— in the school and as a consequence there is hardly any break in continuation and performance of any programme of activities. The pupils are well-directed to undergo the diverse learning programmes according to the school time-table.

(iii) The school time-table is a selected and well-planned chart of work-schedule to systematically set the manifold activities of the school in motion. The allotment of duties are well-planned and, as such, both the teacher and the pupil do not require any forewarning to complete any programme of activity in a disciplined pattern, As the activities and the name of the teacher to guide and supervise these activities are well spelt out, the pupils can chalk out beforehand their approach to performing such activities in a more interesting and planned way. The school time-table, indeed, is an invaluable determinant of all the activities of the school to be performed in a well-spread out and properly balanced manner.

Classification of the School time-table

In organising the activities of the school, different types of the School Time-Table as follows may be introduced:

The General Time-Table

As the name of suggests, the General Time-Table sets forth all the programmes of activities in a broad-based way recording everything in detail. A look at such a time-table prepares one to visualize and assume the total concept of a school in organisation and supervision of the numerous programmes of activities. In fact, it allows one to initially formulate one's opinion of the actual role of the school as a centre of advancement in qualitative education.

The Time-Table for Co-Curricular Activities

The School Time-Table for co-curricular Activities is constructed on the basis of different co-curricular activities including the school functions and festivals to be arranged and organised in an effective way. Here, too, it is framed in accordance with priorities in co-curricular activities to be introduced in a regular and disciplined manner and the assignments of both the teachers and the taught along with the nature and objectives of such activities are displayed in a judicious and synoptic way. Sometimes the role of outside agencies like the community and other specific organisations is also well indicated in this time-table.

The Vacant period Time-Table

The Vacant period Time-Table deals with the programme of activities assigned to teachers for the period lying vacant due to absence of the teacher concerned. This type of time-table arrests indiscipline and chaos that may take place for vacant periods. Sometimes adequate directions are given by means of this time-table to adjust vacant periods to library or laboratory work and so on.

The Special Time-Table

The time-table designated as such covers the following types of time-tables:

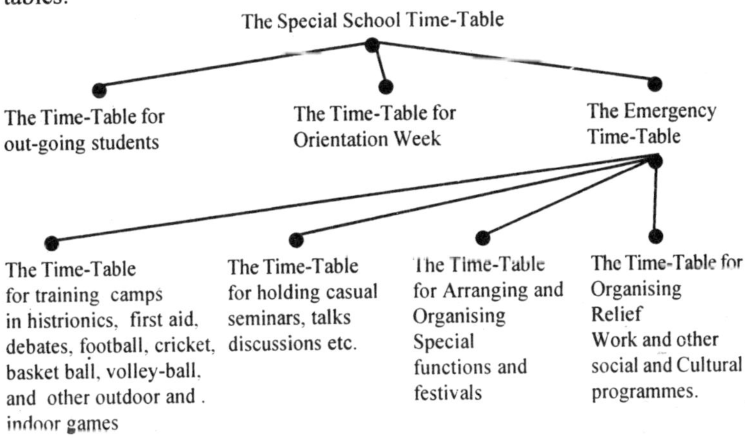

The School Time-Table: Principles of Construction

What are the essential principles of construction of an ideal school time-table? How can those principles be translated and organised? Undeniably, organisation of qualitative school education greatly demands the essential characteristics of a school time-table as follows:—

The first and foremost principle of construction of the school time-table is that it must be *dynamic*. As such, all organisational activities should have a systematic and disciplined continuity and everyone takes interest in his own assignments as a pupil, teacher or organiser.

The principle of *flexibility* should also be maintained in constructing a school time-table. This principle allows necessary changes in the time-table when occasions demand for greater interest of pupils in particular.

The principle of flexibility in the school time-table also directs us to the principle of *revision.* In constructing a time-table enough scope should be there to review it, if necessary. Otherwise, it would be mechanical, dull, drab and passive. None associated with it would respond spontaneously.

Based on the principle of effective and reliable distribution of work, the school time-table should be so constructed as to make it possible for maximum utilization of school library, laboratory, equipments, rooms and the total school complex. This leads us to the principle of *economy* in the construction of the school time-table.

Side by side the above, the principle of *catering to the individual needs and requirements of every pupil* should also be taken into serious consideration. In fact, in organising a school time-table the first acid test should be whether it is aimed at fulfilling and effectively contributing to the all-round development of personality of each and every learner. A good time-table looks after the needs of the advanced pupils and at the same time nursles the requirements of the average and the below average learners. With provisions of extra-classes as indicated in a special time-table, the school can organise separate programmes of teaching the gifted or the backward pupils within or after usual school hours of study.

In constructing an ideal school time-table the principle of *adjustability* should be carefully looked into. This is necessary for organisation of school activities in an effective and judicious manner. Adjustment to local conditions and community needs in a more or less flexible and comprehensive way goes a long way in successful organisation of school education. At the same time, it also saves wastage of space, time and energy.

The principle of *variety* is also important for framing an ideal school time-table. With this principle aptly introduced, the school can organise different forms of activities suited to the needs of varied learning experiences of pupils. The teachers also find an added interest, along with the regular and arduous responsibility of teaching the learners and in familiarizing the latter with newer concepts and experiences.

The principle of *necessity* is a fundamental component to be bourne in mind in framing a school time-table. As a matter of fact, no time-table failing to qualify as an essential tool for organising the school activities should be introduced.

Last but not the least, the school time-table should be constructed in keeping with the *aims and objective of teaching learning programmes* which are subject to *change* for the greater interest of the learning clienteles. If it well responds to aiming at total growth of pupils and maximum spurt for teacher in providing learners with best interests and avenues of appreciation, it proves its effectiveness in organisation of school education.

The principles of framing a school time-table as set forth above are necessary pre-conditions to organising a school effectively. These principles serve as shields against all forms of indiscipline and irregularities in school organisation, supervision, guidance and administration. Today's school education demands all these principles to be strictly carried out in constructing the time-table since pupils at this stage pass the most vital and formative years of life and development of personality and character. Organisation of different programmes of activities can also be smoothly and efficiently made. From all these points of view, it can be unhesitatingly concluded that for organisation of qualitative education— education for excellence and ascent of mankind— the principles of framing a school time-table should be translated into reality as far as practicable.

The School Time-Table: A Tool for Organising Value-based Education

From the organisational points of view, the School time-table has, of late, been considered an essential tool to disseminate value-based education. In this connection, we may consider the following statement made by the Committee for Review of National Policy on Education, 1986:

> There is enough attention paid to the development of the individual through education. The social development of education necessitates that education be essentially value-based. There cannot be an education that is neutral or of a uniform type. Hence there cannot be an educational process and objectives that would fit every people and every nation. Education has to be culturally coloured and enriched. We may view culture from three levels of depth: (a) the superficial or external level gives a sense of identity to a community, group, region or nation. In our case, the different kinds distinctive dresses, the way birth, marriage or death rites are performed by different groups, food preferences and preparations, celebration of festivals etc. fall into this category or level. (b) at a deeper second level, the more substantive aspects of a culture and its achievements are to be found, such as the different dance forms, music traditions, art and architecture, literature, as well as planning, systems of management etc. (c) at the third or deepest

level lie the foundational values, world-views, perspectives, mind-sets, and the philosophy of a people about the view basic realities of life, relations and after life.

Towards and Enlightened and Humane Society

Report of the Committee for Review of National Policy on Education, 1986, Final Report, December 1990, Ministry of Human Resource development, New Delhi 23.

How far is the school time-table justified to the above for effective school organisation?

17

ORGANISATION OF RELATIONSHIPS

Organisation of school education entirely depends on organisation of relationships among the headmaster, the staff, the students and the parents. A healthy organisation of relationships among them assures a healthy school and classroom climate where teaching and learning guarantee qualitative improvement and excellence. Moreover, such organisation of relationships caters to nursling of individuality which is a very important factor for development of pupil-personality. A well-organised plan of activities in school education where individual differences are appreciated and caressed in terms of qualitative development also ensures sharing of common responsibilities so badly needed for conjoint advanced community. Today's school education cannot but be interested in undertaking this responsibility to organise different strategies for maintaining and enriching a healthy relationship among pupils, parents, teachers and the head of the institution which ultimately plays a major role in preparing pupils as members of a global society in future.

The problem of organisation of relationships is essentially related to the problems of organisation of the school environment, the task and the structure with which all activities and programmes are determined. Co-ordination of the school by an 'invisible administrative apparatus' as William Tyler refers to his exposition of the organisation of the school from sociological perspectives may serve as a guideline to organisational relationship.

> The picture of the school as an 'egg create', composed of segregated class-rooms, co-ordinated by an invisible administrative apparatus, is perhaps in keeping with the classical bureaucratic model. For today's schools it is rather misleading at least. Not only have schools evolved multiple layers of interdependence and communication,

they have also increased in size— to the extent that a comprehensive high school of over 1,000 pupils is no longer a rarity. At the same time schools have diversified into a range of specialised units that further compartmentalise and fragment their environment into more manageable sections. Attempts to discover the genesis of local school bureaucracies to some extent may, therefore, miss one of the more immediate problems of school organisation, the features of the task environment which led to structural changes. If we were to ignore for the moment the larger problems of state educational systems and concentrate on the more concrete, contingent and practical aspects of school life, we may develop deeper insights into organisational processes.

— William Tyler : *School Organisation: A Sociological Perspective,* Croom Helm Ltd., London, 1988, p.65.

The Teacher and the Headmaster

The organisational relationship between the teacher and the Headmaster necessitates a newer approach to enlivening school education. At present both of them enjoy islands of alienation. While the teacher remains devoted to the teaching of pupils in different classrooms at different periods scheduled in the school time-table, the headmaster hardly cares for academic activities in most cases and more or less acts like a public relations officer maintaining control and contact with the outside agencies including the school managing committee, the District School Board, the community, the education board, the department of education and so on. A certain sense of alienation thus established between the teacher and the headmaster makes organisational relationship strained and fussy. As a matter of fact, when the teacher meets the headmaster or *vice versa,* administrative issues rather than academic ones become prominent and desirable.

As an organiser it is the duty and responsibility of the headmaster to find out the best way of negotiating the wills and aspirations of a teacher and provide him with all the opportunities for making experimentations with diverse educational problems. He cannot but place before the latter an image of confidence and dependence. Added to this, the following also demand adequate attention and consideration:

(i) The organisational relationship between the headmaster and the teacher should be based on a sense of unity and solidarity.

"United we stand, divided we fall" so goes the proverb, and this is perfectly applicable to better organisation of relationship between the headmaster and the teacher. There should be a greater sense of cooperation and sympathy for understanding, appreciating and evaluating different plans and programmes of activities.

(ii) The school organisational healthfulness is already indicated by the role of the headmaster in giving to and sharing diverse responsibilities with, the teacher. This means that there should be an organised endeavour between them to share different problems of the school.

(iii) There should also be an organised effort at understanding and appreciating mutual role and each of them should enjoy legitimate confidence in discharge of duties. This is greatly lacking in complex school organisation. With gradual increase of teachers and pupils in schools, the thread of organisational relationship between the teacher and the headmaster is gradually becoming loose and even insecure.

(iv) The problems of dishonesty, parochial approach, malpractice, corruption and other moral issues have a great deal affected both the headmaster and the teacher in an era of consumerist and utilitarian approach to school education. This shoots forth in an ugly manner when the headmaster safeguards his teacher even where justice from organisational points of view demands immediate and rigorous action. That there is a certain sense of alienation between the teacher and the headmaster is due to lack of organisational harmony based on discipline, justice and morality.

The catchment areas for organisation of a healthy relationship between the headmaster and the teacher may be identified as follows:

* Curriculum guidance and lesson plans.
* Grouping of pupils for specialized teaching-learning programmes.
* Use of text-books, maps, charts, and other types of teaching aids — visual, audio and audio-visual.

* Use of evaluational programmes.
* Introducing standardized tests in different disciplines.
* Re-thinking institutional features like promotion, system of grading and so on.
* Revaluation of day-to-day programmes of activities curricular as well as co-curricular.
* Individual teacher's work schedule.

Perhaps the most fundamental bond of relationship between the headmaster and the teachers lies in organisation of an effective programme of curriculum guidance and lesson plans. Curriculum as such remains dull and drab both to the teacher and to the learners. The thrilling avenues of functional curriculum necessitate a dynamic approach to activities both inside and outside the classroom. The lesson plans the teacher formulates and works out in the class-room at different periods in different classes or grades encompass diverse activities where organisation of administrative discipline and control demands a mutual understanding and cooperation between the teacher and the headmaster. If the relationship between them is healthy and cordial, the activities get a smooth line of approach where the teacher exercises freedom in imparting instructions to pupils and suggests newer courses of action-programmes for efflorescence of pupil-creativity and critical thinking. In organising lesson plans for group activities, the headmaster may exercise his pivotal role as an effective synchronizer. He arranges for necessary conveyance and funds from outside agencies like the local community or the District School Board and boosts the programme of activities in arranging a rapport between the teachers and the representatives of the concerned agencies.

In grouping of pupils for specialized teaching-learning programmes the joint endeavour of the headmaster and the teachers serves better. Here, too, the former cares and controls the administrative machinery in such a way that the latter find no constraint in translating very intricate and specialized programmes for teaching. The learners, too, enjoy an altogether different instructional climate that inspires them in learning and discovering newer avenues of knowledge and experiences.

To organise and introduce teaching aids in class-rooms the teachers and the headmaster can jointly undertake responsibilities. While in selection of appropriate teaching aids their joint endeavour is necessary, in supply of the same the latter as an organiser makes adequate arrangements in time. A joint endeavour in inspecting and examining the reliability, validity and appropriateness of used up teaching aids also caters to promotion of qualitative teaching in actual class-room atmosphere.

The headmaster comes closer to the teacher when the latter is assured of the fact that he really plays his role as an ideal organiser and takes special interest in introducing good text-books in the school. Organisation of seminars, workshops etc. for teachers from time to time to discuss and evolve newer strategies for introducing qualitative improvement in text-books is one of the major functions of the headmaster. He should also participate in these programmes sincerely, since his role as a teacher in the class-rooms is undeniable.

To chalk out programmes of supervision, the headmaster as an organiser proves his worth most in the crucial discharge of duties in evaluation of pupils. Holding tests, arranging scrutinies for answer scripts, maintaining discipline, declaring results, deciding on admission and transfer, announcing the new session of activities— all these are test items for him as an organiser. If he makes a fairly administrative and supervised control with the assistance of teachers and pupils, he can bring about a remarkable change in teaching-learning atmosphere. As regards the system of grading and day-to-day curricular and co-curricular activities, his dynamic suggestions ably substantiated and supported by teachers pay worthy dividends in course of effective organisation in principles and practice of education.

The headmaster and the teacher come closer together when they mutually share responsibilities in translating individual teacher's work-schedule into reality. Admittedly, it is the teacher who best feels the pulse of every learner in a class-room. But, then, all experimentations and suggestions with regard to improvements in pupil-learning await organisational support and solidarity by the headmaster. If the latter allows freedom for the former to exercise for advancement of pupil-learning, the former finds an added inspiration in carrying out innovative programmes of teaching pupils.

To learn how to organise constraints into opportunities determines the role of the headmaster as an organiser. As such, he makes a joint endeavour with the teacher to eliminate all obstinacies in teaching-learning programmes in action. As an organiser, the headmaster cannot but be concerned with the following work realities:

(a) Haphazard and non-specific feedback programmes are often launched by teachers for pupils. These programmes often remain unknown to the headmaster for reasons beyond his control.

(b) Motivational shortcoming exhibited in the classroom or outside the classroom by external agents, where organisational hazards bring forth professional risks.

(c) Variety and fragmentation of activities together with unusual shortening of work-schedule prepared by teachers for pupils often stand in the way of proper organisational assessments by the headmaster.

(d) Absence of frequent normal opportunities in sharing the experiences of teachers often leads not to have a comprehensive account of the work-reality and teacher-competency by the headmaster as an organiser of education.

(e) A comparative approach to teacher competency as well as that of the headmaster among all the neighbouring schools which clearly reveals a total picture of organisational relationship can hardly be undertaken and this organisational constraint severely tells upon sound and healthy relationship. In fact, this workreality has its graver perspectives to be assessed in terms of disintegration writ large among teachers and headmasters in rural and urban schools.

(f) Organisation of a viable relationship between the headmaster and the teacher from the standpoint of professional growth and excellence in innovative programmes of teaching demands a greater bond of cohesion. The headmaster should enjoy the additional administrative power to exercise in this direction.

(g) To support and strengthen work-ability and work-enrichment, the headmaster may be allowed to delegate authority to the teachers either individually or jointly to share organisational responsibility. This ensures organisational elasticity and flexibility that eliminate class-consciousness in educational administration and supervision. The teachers really consider the headmaster as a crucial and cordial partner to advancement in teaching-learning programmes of activities.

In connection with effective organisational relationship between the headmaster and the teacher, the following table shows how the headmaster in association with the teacher can significantly contribute to school improvement form diverse points of view:

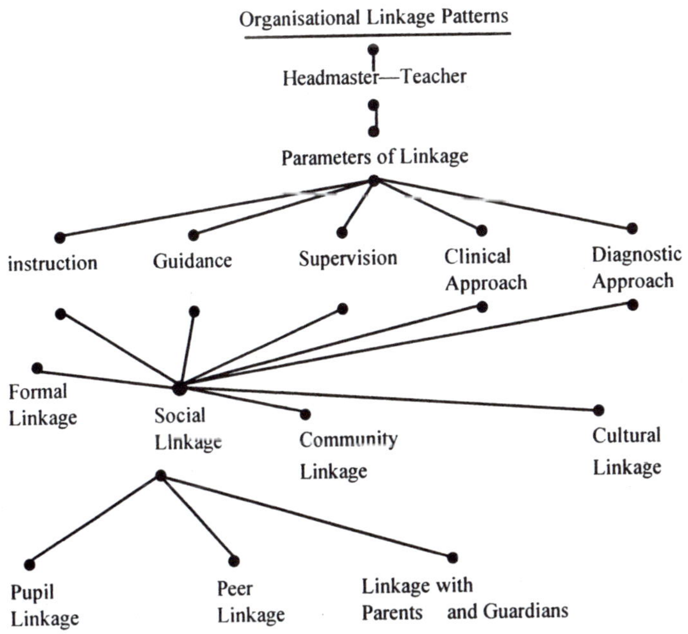

A study of the different parameters of linkage between the headmaster and the teacher from the points of view of organisation of education as shown in the table above pre-supposes the following essential components:

(a) A wide and liberal provision for teachers to impart instructions to pupils.

(b) Sufficient scope for directing and channelizing guidance programmes for pupils.

(c) Distribution of work in supervision programmes for pupils. Allowance of evaluation and self-supervision programmes for pupils.

(d) Locating clinical cases where concerned pupils are to be taught after ascertaining actual educational, administrative and supervisory programmes specially designed to meet their needs.

(e) Finalising diagnostic programmes for concerned pupils for educational progress. Preparation of teachers to be equipped with the required skill for appropriate diagnostic research to arrest abuse of pupil-personality.

In this connection, it is interesting to note that the observations of teachers in any of the essential components as referred to above should be seriously taken into consideration by the headmaster. Otherwise there might be a break in the organisational linkage between them.

Alteration of work-structures plays a significant role in the interplay of ideas and activities of teachers. The headmaster as a foreseer organises different programmes to harmonize inter-relationship among them. He also makes a thorough probe into their mutual feelings and appreciation of better work-cultures. The different perspectives of organisation in this connection may be analysed as follows:

(a) The head of the institution should be blessed with available resources in the three-fold manner— materials, money and enough time— to combat organisational deadlocks.

(b) Provision for application of unused skills forms an integral part of class-room teaching. The headmaster should have opportunities for allowing his teachers to explore this avenue by means of innovation and experimentation.

(c) A reshuffled approach to in-service activities and training programmes for teachers forms an indispensable part of qualitative teaching. The headmaster as a practical organiser of school education cannot but nursle this principle both in theory and in practice.

(d) To maintain and cherish a positive public view of the school as an organised seat of learning in the midst of discipline and punctuality, the headmaster should set an example of how to restore and highlight the sanctity and prestige of the school. Then the teachers and the pupils enjoy teaching and learning in a disciplined atmosphere. The headmaster also acts as a comrade to the teachers and guide to the pupils in diverse teaching-learning programmes.

(e) As an indispensable communicator of culture, the headmaster seeks all kinds of assistance form the teachers who organise different functions and festivals which expose the co-curricular activities backed by experience and beneficial turnouts. As an all-time on-looker of school activities, he identifies the constraints of the teacher devoted to such programmes of activities and lends as best as possible from the organisational points of view a helping hand to make each programme a thrilling success.

(f) Grouping of pupils for better organisation of class-room teaching is a psychological activity in terms of pupil behaviour. The headmaster as an organiser joins hands with the teacher in the latter's endeavour at better and more justified grouping of pupils keeping in view the psychological theory of individual differences amongst them and also bearing in mind the principle of individualizing instructions but socializing the pupils at the same time. A slight change in the pattern of classification, if well organised and introduced, brings forth very good results in advancement of learning. The headmaster holds this principle high above anything in school education but as a practical organiser seeks persistent and strong support from the teachers whom he assists from every possible aspect. As a key actor in organisation of school activities he stands by the side of every teacher-colleague who chalks out innovative programmes of class-teaching by exercising authority and freedom in discharge of duties. The break-up of pupils according to their skills, abilities, interests and so on and imparting instructions thereto find a strong and positive support from the headmaster as a dynamic organiser.

As is the headmaster so is the school. This proverbial statement is justified when in addition to organisation of formal linkage between the headmaster and the teacher, other parameters of linkages like social, community and cultural ones are maintained. Pupil linkage, peer-linkage and linkage with parents and guardians also significantly contribute to healthy organisation.

The teacher-headmaster relationship essentially hangs on the fine balance of mutual cooperation in organisation of school education. The finer sensibilities and the softer visions of the teacher are often left uncared for and unassessed by the headmaster who remains burdened with administrative and supervisional activities. Just as well-directed organising abilities also demand a subjective approach for the headmaster to negotiate pupil-problems so also is the need for a personal approach whereby he comes closer to the teachers as his partners to progress in school education. A little sense of appreciation, empathy and earnestness judiciously applied to negotiate the diverse problems of the teachers goes a long way in establishing a harmonious bond of relationship between the headmaster and the teacher.

Relationships: The Teacher and the Pupils

The teacher holds a very importants position in the organisational activities of the school. As are the teachers so is the school— so goes the proverb. As the teacher comes directly in contact with the students regularly, the major duties and responsibilities related to classroom and school organisation are executed by him. If he is sincerely devoted to the manifold educational and other allied problems of his pupils and organises special programmes of activities designed to meet their tendencies and motivation, the latter find a new spurt of enthusiasm in pursuit of education and honour the teacher as a genuine guide to all-round development of personality. If, on the other hand, the teacher, as an organiser, fails to ignite his pupils with the right approach to advancement of learning and leaves the latter to be guided by mere whims and caprices, they become prone to indiscipline— a common experience in present day schools suffering from lopsided organisation and administration— and a strained relationship unfortunately develops beyond control. Therefore, it is undeniable that all attention in school education should be geared to disciplined school organisation in general, and a healthy and effective organisation of relationship between the teacher and the pupils in particular.

Organisational Avenues

To facilitate better relationship between the teacher and the pupils the following organisational avenues may be considered:

(a) To stimulate pupils to be fair minded in their approach to creative and critical thinking.

(b) To enable pupils to develop within themselves the healthy spirit of refined generalisations.

(c) To allow pupils to clarify ideas, issues and problems by inspiring them to raise and pursue root questions and develop the spirit of positive enquiry.

(d) To encourage pupils to enrich standards of judgment in every item of learning and experience.

(e) To equip pupils to go ahead with newer theories and experimentations by supplying them with evidence and reasons.

(f) To associate pupils with real life experiences and encounter diversifications thereof.

(g) To explore newer possibilities of sharing community life in association with culture.

Admittedly, plans and programmes, rules and regulations in connection with school organisation are determined and chalked out from ivory towers, but it is the humble teacher, dissociated from all these and devoted to earnestly implement these theories in practice in the actual class-room situation, who cares more for pupils' growth and development of personality.

A cordial and healthy relationship between the teacher and the pupils develop through understanding and appreciation of social values. The teacher as an organiser of co-curricular activities teaches pupils the fundamental social values so necessary for fullness of man. It is the teacher who actually highlights the school as a social system. A historical approach to teacher autonomy and functionalist theory so far as school organisation is concerned better identifies teacher-pupil relationship. As Tyler observes:

> The relationships between headmasters and teachers and those between teachers and pupils are subject to more or less the same institutional constraints in the moral and technical modes by which autonomy might be constituted and exercised.
>
> ★ ★ ★
>
> The more recent types of school organisation would therefore not be more rationally organised or necessarily more evolved than the earlier. Certain kinds of technology can change, but the same fundamental impression of goals and uncertainties in the technology world prevails. Thus the imputation of greater autonomy, in any of these dimensions would probably be either denied or questioned. Interactionists, by the same token, would look critically at these organisational types and theoretically defined stages but would view them as reifications of social process. A Structuralist would also inject some greater degree of indeterminacy into the relationships between the formal theory of structural evolution and the situated meanings of teachers and students.
>
> — William Tyler: *School Organisation: A Sociological Perspective,* Croom Helm Limited, London 1988, pp. 40-41.

For organisation of challenging teaching that consolidates relationship between the teachers and the taught, consistency among teachers plays a very significant role. There must be an inherent relationship among teachers in imparting instructions. This enables pupils to be assured of learning objectives and learning parameters. A well organised school maintains this inherent relationship and enables pupils to save unnecessary time and energy. Absence of repetition of teaching items by different teachers also ensures organisational clarity of relationship between the teacher and the pupil.

On the threshold of a new era of school education, organisational relationship plays a very significant role in teacher efficiency and pupils performance. Moreover, education always awaits dynamic leadership where the whole school with the members of the staff and pupils act like a joint, happy and well-disciplined family. School organisation should be geared to this fundamental end in view to thrust forward an enlightened humane society. Does every school substantially contribute to this end in view?

18

ORGANISATION OF CO-CURRICULAR ACTIVITIES

School education is greatly dependent on organisation of co-curricular activities. These activities ensure dynamism in the total school complex. Everyone associated with teaching and learning in a school feels a sense of living and thrilling atmosphere in the event of activities going on inside or outside the class-room. Unless there are activities for the teachers as well as for the pupil, the school loses its functional role and becomes dead and silent. The voice of the school is the voice of motion, the voice that proclaims the spirit of activity and dynamism. As a living organ of teaching and learning, it demands an organised platform of education through work. Modern psychologists pay maximum importance to this psychological approach to children's education in particular.

Prior to making a broadbased discussion on organisation of co-curricular activities, a spell-out of concepts like activity and curriculum becomes all the more necessary.

What is an activity? It is, to define categorically, a part of development. Children in schools are engaged in different types of activities primarily because these would lead to specific forms of development. If they are not directed to be interested and take part in different forms of activities, their education would become meaningless. If, on the other hand, they are instructed to learn through activities, learning becomes psychological and effective.

There are two stages of activity: one, the physical stage of activity, and the other, the psychological one. The former leads the learner to physical development, the latter encourages him to mental development. A psycho-social development of the learner is greatly needed for worthy citizenship of the future.

The stages of activity as referred to above are carefully natured by means of a well-organised ploicy of importing instruction. These stages may be elucidated in the tabular form as follows :

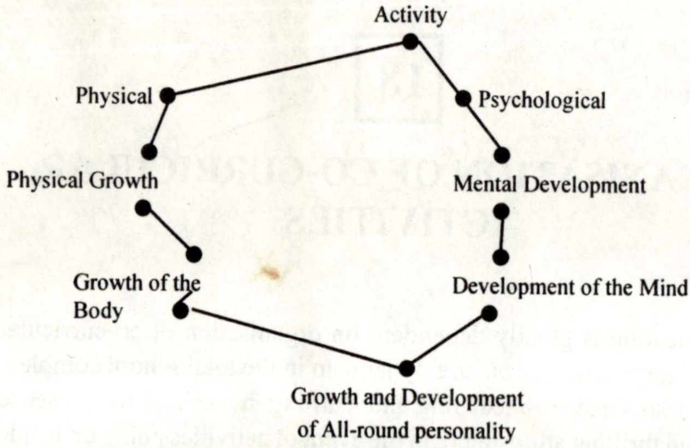

Admittedly, organisation of activities in school is primarily based on the axiom that each activity is a part of development. If there is no activity, there is no scope for development.

Considering the above fundamental theory of development, modern school education heavily banks upon learning by doing. The emotional development of the learner is possible through participation in activities. Curriculum is actually a blend of subject and activity. If there is not scope for organisation of activity, curriculum becomes partial and incomplete as it barely deals with dead subjects.

As organisation of curriculum is actually organisation of subject plus activity, the cohesion, between being and doing contributes to the total development of the child. The facilitate organisation of activity, school education also incorporates co-curricular activities—which ultimately mingle with the curriculum. So activities-curricular, co-curricular or extra-curricular— are in the end in absolute conformity with organisation of education for being and doing which as indicated below, leads to total development of the learner.

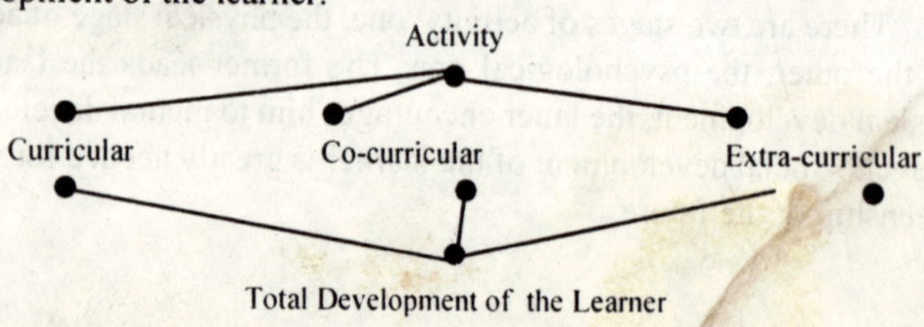

Historical Background

Are co-curricular activities introduced in schools a very recent strategy for better organisation of education? Or, are these based on a sound historical background? A historical survey of school education gives a positive and clear response to the latter.

Organisation of activities in education is nothing new. In Persia, Sparta, Athens and Rome, athletic exercises were activities which formed an important part in educational fundamentals. The history of the Olympic games also bears witness to this fact. In the Mediaeval period, activities were organised in education in almost the same way. The Greek chorus supplemented by the choir-boys, students and others and headed by a procession of monks leads education to a doing project. The forming of guilds in Bologna and the practice of Hazing particularly popular as a co-curricular activity in German universities also bears witness to organisation of education as an activity. We also come across a special activity introduced in the form of student handbooks specially designed to be handled and exercised by pupils regularly.

Organisation of co-curricular activities in England dates back from 1383 when direct evidence of participation of pupils can be found in the statutes framed for Winchester College. Supervision programmes were conducted by entrusting these scholars of good character with the duties and responsibilities of maintaining discipline through work.

As a part of curriculum, training in histrionics was organised in Shrewbury, England. Education thus becomes functional and interesting. Vittrnrino de Feltre recommended drawing as a co-curricular activity to make the learning of history and geometry living and engrossing. Programmes of learning were so organised that the curriculum became dynamic through introduction of a series of activities. As a co-curricular activity of sustained interest, singing in elementary and secondary schools has now become widely popular. The monitorial system introduced by Malim of Eton around 1561 is also an accepted pattern of school organisation that is based on the principle of education through work. Pestalozzi's significant contribution to education as a psychological process is even now considered a major step in organisation of school education by means of incorporation and introduction of co-curricular activities. Till now, no education apart from the principle of learning by doing which forms an essential component on co-curricular activities becomes effective and interesting.

The different types of co-curricular activities organised and introduced in schools may be analysed as follows:

The School Assembly

This is an important co-curricular activity. The programmes of the school assembly are formulated and organised by pupils themselves in consultation with the teacher in charge as and when necessary. The pupils are allowed to exercise their own strategies suited best for organisation and management of the school assembly. This also forms an essential part of the school time table. A particular period specially on the first or the last working day of the week is is earmarked for the school Assembly. Records of programmes organised in the assembly are carefully and sincerely maintained regularly by pupils themselves. Sometimes they are verified and countersigned by the teacher in charge or the president of each assembly programme.

From the organisational point of view, the school assembly does not require any special arrangement. The infrastructure of the school is enough for its smooth organisation. Normally every school has an assembly hall which can be very well utilized for the purpose.

Departmental Clubs

Organising departmental clubs like science club, history club etc. allow pupils to have an exercise of theoretical knowledge in different subjects into practice. The science clubs are specially organised to enhance pupil-participation in science show, science museum and and exhibition on science. Special science week may be observed in the school and eminent scientists may be invited on such an occasion. The history clubs also stimulate pupils to prepare maps, charts, date lines of historical events etc., which enable them to have an extensive approach to the study of history from the practical and functional points of view.

Publication Activities

Organisation of publication activities like publishing the school magazine develops cultural and aesthetic sensibilities among pupils. They are entrusted with duties and responsibilities like collecting of articles, poems etc., arranging them after proper selection and editing with the assistance of teachers concerned.

Different types of school magazines like the Annual School Magazine, Subject-wise Wall Magazine, Class-wise School Magazine etc. can be effectively organised with a little bit of planning, guidance and supervision. The students may also be introduced with the latest trends and techniques in publication by arranging and organising a visit to the newspaper offices and press and publicity departments of governmental or non-governmental organisations.

Social Activities

Organisation of co-curricular activities also includes each item like holding a picnic, making a short trip, arranging educational excursions which come under the purview of social activities. Through organisation of these types of co-curricular activities, pupils learn the lesson of co-operation, sympathy, sharing of ideas and experiences, unity and other qualities related to sociability. Careful organisation of these activities undoubtedly leads to learning economy, self-help and the lesson of good citizenship. It is heartening to note that modern school education is particularly taking keen interest in the organisational aspects of these types of co-curricular activities.

Pupil Participation in Public Systems

As promising would be citizen of future, pupils are directed to act as disciplinarians and exponents of law and order by means of service as traffic controllers and firefighting personnels. These highly specialized assignments become thrilling to the young learner provided that these are well-organised. Experienced traffic personnels and experts in road safety may also be invited for the purpose of worthwhile demonstration.

Community Service

Organisation of Community Service programmes may be one of the most functional co-curricular school activities. Pupils enjoy community living and community performance and learn important community living habits by involving themselves in the nursing of the aged and infirm, assisting the visually disadvantaged and the disabled, joining community health and sanitation service and helping people to be literate and happy partners to national progress and solidarity.

Social Days

Observing special days like the Republic Day, the Independence Day etc. in a befitting manner accelerates pupil-awareness to nationalism and humanism. Such types of co-curricular activities demand a systematic co-ordination in organisation. If the pupils are divided into a few groups and allocation of duties is made in accordance with the abilities, testes and temperaments, pupils find an altogether newer lease of life in discharging their duties with a serene sense of patriotism. Education then becomes an action *per excellence.*

Athletics and Sports

Athletics and sports form a special type of co-curricular activities and if these are well-organised, pupils learn the lesson of cultivation of physical health for enrichment and excellence of mental health. They also learn the value of the maxim that a sound mind resides only in a sound body. They learn the right use of time, steadfastness, co-operation and unity by participating in school games and sports.

Musical Activities

Co-curricular activities related to music impress upon the minds of the young learners in schools. When these are organised, this particular end-in-view is sincerely considered. Musical competitions, if organised well, stimulate the finer sensibilities and the aesthetic temperaments of competitors. The teacher in charge of organising such activities often actively participates in the different programmes sponsored by the pupils themselves. An organised musical programme also facilitates the school administrative authorities to be rest assured with the spontaneous role of each pupil participant. As discipline here is free and natural, pupils come forward to be associated with such activities in a voluntary manner. Thus the school choir or the school band team takes up the charge of smooth functioning of the school's daily prayer and other functions and festivals. The school musical drill unit is also spontaneously formed by eager pupils who also learn themselves how to be habituated with the spirit of regularity, discipline and group activity.

Organisation of musical activities in school education has also its other invaluable aspect. These activities may be geared to arouse the spirit of national and global awareness. Programmes may be chalked out to cater to the needs of pupils of different age groups and musical activities may be introduced in the stipulated period earmarked in the school table.

Recreational Activities

Recreational activities as co-curricular activities abundantly appear to pupils in schools. These activities, if well organised, lessen the burden of the curriculum heavily thrust upon them and simplify instructional strategies of the teachers in class-rooms. Moreover, some lessons are more adequately and judiciously taught by means of recreational activities than by imparting instructions in the class-room.

Among popular recreational activities which deserve mention for organisation in schools, circus shows, dramatic performances, magic shows and so on are really interesting to pupils. These co-curricular activities also supplement and enrich the theoretical lesson of the curriculum already learnt in the class-room in the routinized periods of study. Moreover, the exercise of freedom of activity for the learner so limited and very often absent from the curricular activities in the day to day class-room study is liberally allowed in co-curricular activities of the recreation types as above. Histrionic experts may be invited to practically demonstrate dramatic techniques, explain stagecraft artistry and set before pupils living examples in role playing by means of participation with the pupils. Sometimes open-air dramatic performances during leisure hours may also be organised with limited participants of a particular class or a group of classes. In organising such co-curricular activities care should be taken to see that pupils may not be overenthusiastic and emotional at the cost of losing attention and devotion to regular curricular activities.

Speech Activities

Organisation of speech activities as forms of co-curricular activities serves as an important medium of consolidation of theoretical learning in the class-rooms. The aims and objectives of oral work can be effectively derived through learning outcomes in the programmes of co-curricular activities related to the skill of speaking. The essentials and techniques of speech activities can be exercised by means of organising the following forms of speech activities in school education:

(a) Debates

The school may organise of debating society wherein the fundamentals of the art of debating may be exercised. The rules and regulations of holding a debate may be discussed and practically demonstrated by the teacher-in-charge. The school debating team may be allowed to participate in inter-school debating competitions through which rich experiences may be achieved. Normally, the senior students of a school can be instructed to organise debates amongst themselves.

(b) Discussions/Seminars/Symposia

Speech activities in the forms of discussion, seminars, symposia and so on may also be organised in schools. The matter for discussion or for the seminar or the symposium may be appropriately and judiciously selected in keeping with the school curricular activities and guidance and supervisions may be thoroughly made.

Eloquence Competition

On the spot speech activities like eloquence competitions, if well organised, may lead to contribute substantially to the advancement of learning. Matters of eloquence tests should be at par with the pupils', standard of knowledge and experience in vocabulary and concepts and the time allotted to the purpose should be judiciously ascertained. In fact, if such eloquence tests as a form of speech activities are effectively introduced, spontaneity and creativity in learning through co-curricular activities become an organised affair of success and fulfilment.

Speech Activities Through Teaching Aids

Speech activities of diverse forms of co-curricular activities may be interestingly performed by means of organising and displaying worthwhile and appropriate teaching aids like pictures, charts, flash cards etc. Care should be taken in selection of such teaching aids. As an ideal technique of organisation of such speech activities, teachers may themselves prepare graded matters for display for each pupil-participant. The former may display the matter before the latter with or without an introduction and instruct to describe the same orally within a stipulated period of time. If necessary, cues may be supplied and corrections may be made instantly or afterwards. Models for such activities may be presented by inviting experts.

Celebrating Special Days

Organisation of co-curricular activities commemorating special days like the Republic Day, the National Independence Day, birthdays of eminent persons and so on has, of late, become a regular feature in school education. A little bit of sincerity and disciplined approach to such co-curricular activities can pay thrilling rewards in the forms of exercise of the spirit of national consciousness, patriotism, unity, co-operation, patience and sympathy. Exhibitions in connection with celebration of these days may be organised in a planned manner.

Public-Participation in School Control and Administration

Pupils directly participating in school control and administration feel themselves satisfied and glorified in school organisation, because they no longer remain alienated from teachers and school administrators but become a part and parcel of the school from all aspects. Indeed, when pupils are delegated the power to maintain school discipline and regulate law and order, the task of the teacher and the school administrator is half completed and the rest follows smoothly and efficiently. The school that organises school programmes encompassing the duties and responsibilities of pupils to control and administer the school, also provides opportunities for them to exercise their knowledge in practice by taking or teaching in some classes where they are considered fit. This also improves the class-room climate since pupils find that they are being honoured and respected by other pupils of the junior classes wherein they are assigned to teach As the classes are well-organised in this way, the problem of assignment of teaching in the vacant periods are easily and effectively solved.

The time-table for pupil-participation in school control and administration can be successfully introduced in the following ways:

1 *Physical Dimensions*

Name of the Pupil-Participant.. . . . .Class/Section/. . . . .
Class to which assigned. ....
Section
Grade
Group
Name of the school...

Period/Time	Ist	2nd	3rd	4th	5th	6th	7th	8th
	☐	☐	☐	☐	☐	☐	☐	☐

Shift: Morning/Afternoon

Half: 1st ☐ 2 nd ☐

Subject taught................ Topic ....Section I ☐
Part I ☐ II ☐
Date: .... II ☐ III ☐
III ☐

II. Co-curricular Activities

Name of the Activity ....
Type of the Activity ☐ Indoor
☐ Outdoor
Total period of Assignment ....Hours
................Minutes
................Seconds
Instruments/Appliances/Equipment used.....................................
....
Name of the Organiser/Teacher/Guide/Supervisor.........................

		Excellent	Good	Poor
Evaluation Record/ Scale	Performance	☐	☐	☐
	Organising ability	☐	☐	☐
Self-Evaluational Record/ Scale	Performance	☐	☐	☐
	Organising ability	☐	☐	☐

With regard to organisation and maintenance of discipline, pupils may themselves determine and execute plans and programmes. They may formulate their own council in which they may select representatives for the following areas of school organisation in a democratic manner by exercising their power of franchise:

(i) President
(ii) Vice-President
(iii) General Secretary
(iv) Assistant Secretary
(v) Secretary: Games and Sports
(vi) Cultural and Literary Secretary
(vii) Secretary for Social Service
(viii) Secretary for School Health and Sanitation
(ix) Secretary: The School Book Bank
(x) Secretary: The School Publications
(xi) Representatives of different classes

The different portfolios as referred to above are not exhaustive but suggestive and omission or inclusion of any portfolio depends upon the roll-strength of the school and the organising ability of pupils. The number of representatives may also vary from school to school keeping in view the aims and objectives of progressive school organisation.

In this connection, it would perhaps be appropriate to refer to pupil school-control and administration introduced by Rabindranath Tagore in Santiniketan for better organisation of school education. Student's indiscipline in his own school, Patha-Bhavana, is to a great extent negotiated and controlled even now in an incomparably successful way through *Vichar Sabha.* Pupils here spontaneously organise and control cultural and literary activities, games and sports, functions and festivals in joyous and happy unison with their teachers.

Organisational know-whys in co-curricular Activities: A Retrospect

Looking back to organisational know-whys in co-curricular activities normally introduced in schools the fundamental objectives as follows serve as guidelines to better school organisation:

(i) To enable pupils to nursle an adventurous spirit and zest for life.

(ii) To inspire pupils to have a definite quest for knowing the unknown and experience whatever still remains beyond the domain of experience.

(iii) To stimulate pupils to cultivate the spirit of honesty, morality and positive restraint.

(iv) To encourage pupils to exercise their aesthetic sensibilities as manifested in idealizing and experimenting upon Truth, Goodness and Beauty in everyday life.

(v) To stimulate pupils in group activities, group involvement in problems of life and work and encourage them to launch group programmes of enquiry and analysis, comparison and evaluation.

(vii) To boost pupils to develop and exercise freely and profoundly their creative and critical thinking and power of expression.

(vi) To foster amongst pupils an urge for development of positive physical and mental growth and development.

(viii) To show pupils the diverse avenues to self-control in order to be regulated by law and order, discipline and punctuality.

(ix) To accelerate among pupils the spirit of altruism and widen pupil-to-pupil and pupil-to-teacher contact.

(x) To provide pupils with profuse scope for maintenance and nurturing of diverse interaction in opinion and work.

(xi) To allow pupils to be bold enough to accept any challenge in work and its outcome poor or subject to severe criticism. A sense of self-confidence and self-service so badly necessary for development of pupil-personality is always backed in any well organised co-curricular activity.

A few more objectives in connection with organisation of activities may by stated in terms of enquiry as follows:

(a) Do these activities really contribute to organisation of the curriculum in unison of objectives?
(b) Do these activities vitalize learning from every possible point of view?
(c) Are these activities oriented in such a way as to qualify pupils to share responsibilities and undertake risks as and when necessary?
(d) Do these activities positively respond to community problems and involve pupils therein?
(e) Do these activities lead pupils to learn and exercise the spirit of democracy as a positive way of life?
(f) Are these activities genuinely representing the rich heritage of mankind?

Undeniably, each pupil is at the centre of every co-curricular activity and whenever there is a chaos in its organisation, it definitely invites ukase in the school climate. The seeds of disintegration are then in a position to revolt in the absence of proper control and so thrive happily without facing any kind of protest. Behind all incidents of students' unrest in the school campus lies the strong support of indiscipline where organisation in the true sense of the term enjoys unusual slumber. Added to this is a certain sense of passivity which aggravates mismanagement and aimlessness in school organisation. It is really unfortunate that in most schools where organisational loopholes are appalling, teachers and administrators also gradually become victims to— or are immuned to— prolonged passivity.

Amidst this picture of chaos in organisation of schools, let us try to apprise the real position of the learner pupil. He is as it were a stranger to negotiate with some intrinsic and and extrinsic components which can be set as follows:

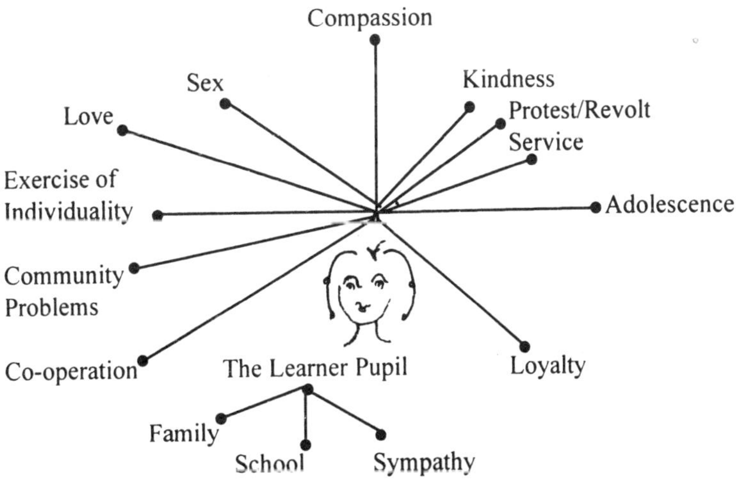

Organisation of co-curricular activities to bring about a futuristic thrust in education particularly at the school level is crucial to the creation of a healthy and strengthened democracy. Let the spirit of work infused in the mind of every young learner be turned into the spirit of worship. Let the idealised system of education so burdened with bare curriculum be tightened with the conjoint endeavour of teachers and pupils sharing and experiencing knowledge in joyous and thrilling co-curricular activities.

Today's promises in organisation of education beckon and assure those of the future. The vision of a better tomorrow rests on the fulfilments of the vision of today. As such, our aims and objectives of dynamic education are entirely related to regular and disciplined organisation of co-curricular activities suited to the growth and development of pupil-personality. Every school within its own limited scope for organisation of co-curricular activities necessitates a pilot study on the use and abuse of infra-structural resources and man-power potentiality. It is, therefore, to be bourne in mind that quality in education primarily depends on quality in organisation and this is perhaps more viable in school education because pupils at this stage pass the most formative and turning period of life. The task of organising co-curricular activities for these pupils is undeniably challenging specially to teachers who best know the trends and traits of pupil-personality while interacting with them in day to day classroom hours. Again, a greater and more positive administrative response to suggestions and remarks on revamping co-curricular activities by teachers demands immediate attention. Do we translate this fact in our programmes for organising co-curricular activities in school education?

19

THE ROLE OF THE HEADMASTER AS A SCHOOL ORGANISER

Organisation of education is a complex activity. It becomes more complex in case of schools where pupils demand continuous and sincere care and attention, guidance and supervision. At the same time, organisation of school education demands teachers to serve as catalysts to whatever is favourable for desirable administration and education. While in the latter there are unipolar responsibilities as mostly apparent, in the former an invisible but more sustained approach to leadership always acts like an enzyme. Hence, the importance of the role of the headmaster as a school organiser.

Who is a headmaster? A quizzical askance, indeed. A headmaster, a principal, a rector, an administrator, an educational leader, organiser, synthesizer, catalyst, co-ordinator, well, one can go on adding to or christening the head of the school in any way one likes but the characteristic definition still remains lacking. This does not, of course, minimize or hamper the vision of a headmaster as an organiser of the school. Rather does it appeal more to our quest for unfolding the image of the headmaster from the right perspective. As a matter of fact, the following serve as evaluational gross components of his organisational leadership:

(i) The headmaster should be a man of high academic distinction and scholar of eminence.

(ii) The physical appearance of the headmaster should be pleasing, handsome, grave but appealing.

(iiii) The headmaster should be a man of character and strong personality.

(iv) The headmaster should have a distinctive role in the school as well as in the community.

(v) The headmaster is able to maintain a cordial relationship with everyone within and outside the school.

(vi) The headmaster should have an organising ability to think, act and devise new methods and approaches to dynamic education.

(viii) The headmaster should have the organising foresight to turn the whole school into a harmonized enlightened humane family of teachers, pupils, parents, guardians and members of the community.

It is interesting to note in this connection that even if all the qualities in the forms of components as referred to above are there in the headmaster, these may not— and, in fact, do not — guarantee his successful role of organising the school. Often it so happens that the headmaster as an organiser discharges his duties more in silence than in direct involvements. But then, to be justified to the aims and objectives of the role of the headmaster as an organiser of school education, the following parameters of organisation may be suggested:

(i) To establish a specific vision that econompasses clear priorities, goals and objectives of education.

(ii) To consolidate the vision in objectives of education to be assured of decision making in every direction of school education.

(iii) To highlight pupil-performance encapsulating every avenue of attitude, interest, appreciation, behavioural design or achievement as best as possible.

(iv) To efficiently and strictly introduce school business affair by ardently following the school time-table. The qualitative improvement in pupil-performance necessitates apt and challenging operation of instructional strategies and this, again, await suggestions to be negotiated by a well-balanced time-table to the organised effectively by the headmaster like the captain of a ship.

(v) To serve as an exponent and disseminator of invaluable opinions and suggestions given by teachers from time to time and to earnestly fulfil their expectations.

(vi) To stimulate pupils through occasional meetings, discussions, talks, participation in games and sports and other co-curricular activities well-organised and favourably situated in individual pupil's tastes and temperaments.

(vii) To be optimistic about pupil-progress and pupil-success in every activity curricular or co-curricular and to stand by them in hours of failure or disappointment, futility and loneliness.

(viii) To be well-communicative in the approach to forge a greater bond of harmony amongst students, staffs, parents and guardians as far as practicable.

(ix) To make a joint endeavour with the members of the community, staff, and students to launch environmental changes in the school climate and safeguard it against hooliganism, anti-social activities and so on detrimental to advancement of learning.

(x) To arrange for discussing with the guardians, parents, students, staff and others associated with the well-being of the school on newer approaches to curriculam development and strategies for introducing co-curricular activities in diverse dimensions suited to the needs and interests of pupils with individual differences.

(xi) To allow teachers to be co-partners sharing equal responsibilities for better school organisation.

(xii) To establish a favourable climate of confidence between the teachers and himself and between the teachers and the pupils in particular.

(xiii) To frankly seek public opinion for better organisation and management of school activities.

(xiv) To set living examples of co-operation and sympathy among all associated with the entire school family.

(xv) To provide teachers with ample opportunities and sufficient resources for school planning and expertise.

(xvi) To invite suggestions for members of the staff to negotiate immediate and crucial bottlenecks in school organisation.

The organising ability of the headmaster depends on maintenance of all round improvement in school education. His efficiency in leadership lies in a balanced synchronization between the instrumental dimension and the expressive dimension of his role as a principal organiser of school activities. As Musgrave elucidates these two dimensions of the role of the headmaster as an organiser:

> The first relates to administrative details and follows from the particular way in which he emphasises and orders the priorities that are inherent in his perception of the task given to the school. This may be called the INSTRUMENTAL dimensions of his role. It will include decision relating to the curriculum, the time-table, external examinations and streaming. The second dimension may be termed EXPRESSIVE and refers to decisions relating to the maintenance of the emotional equilibrium of the staff and pupils. Examples of expressive decisions are the steps taken to smooth quarrels and friction among staff, the arrangement made to ease unpopular changes in rules amongst staff and children, the organisation established to allow parents to see staff, and the facilities provided in the school, whether curricular or extra-curricular, to gain allegiance of the pupils to the goals of the school as the head sees them.

Heads give different emphases to these two dimensions. Thus a head who puts great stress on the instrumental dimension but gives small place to the expressive dimension may be called a martinet, while another head who gives the opposite emphases by stressing the expressive and ignoring the instrumental may be seen as permissive. Various combinations of emphasis are possible and each will result in a different interpretation of the role of head. Each particular style of leadership has an effect on how those outside the organisation see the school and on how closely they identify with it. This in turn could affect the support that, for instance, parents are likely to give to what the head is trying to do for their children. The head's leadership role will also affect the closeness with which his staff relate to the school. It could well be that styles of leadership have immeasurable outcomes — in the case of clients in the rate of drop-out and in the cause of the teachers in the rate of turnover of staff.

— P.W. Musgrave: "The Role of the Head",
The School as an Organiser,
Macmillan, London, 1968, pp. 32-543.

A relational approach to education as the headmaster takes up from instrumental and expressional dimensions has a chained organisational course of action where the school works in unison. This systematic approach is the only alternative to arrest ukase in organisation and administration of school education. This also strengthens the strategic avenues of furtherance of pupil-scholarship and pupil-excellence as teachers themselves are encouraged to formulate and apply innovative principles in the methodologies of teaching different items of interest.

The pivotal role of the headmaster as an educational organiser is best assumed and taken into practical consideration from a study of the relational set-up as shown in the following table:

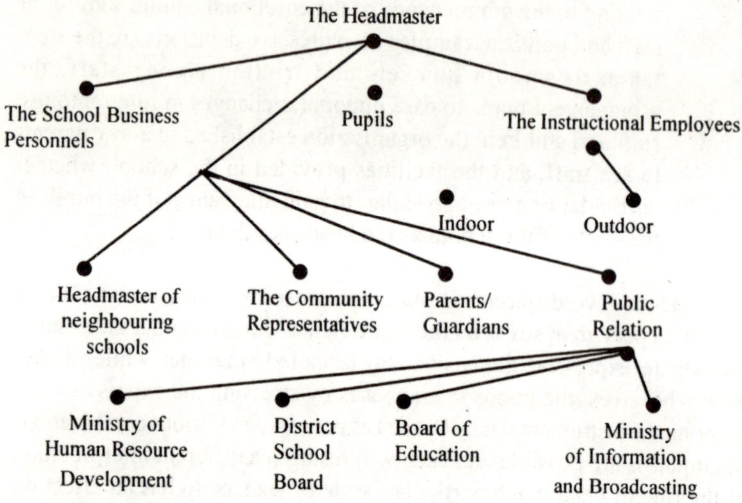

Like a skilful business expert, the headmaster handles the school business personnels who are assigned to look into the school business affairs in day to day school organisation. He makes a thorough study of the school accounts in association with them, discusses on crucial issues like the annual school budgets, probes into organisational anomalies specially related to school administration and suggest avenues for smooth function and control of school business affairs. Admittedly, he is to maintain discipline and punctuality in every matter of school organisation, which ultimately stimulate the entire school community. It is by means of his organising statesmanship that the headmaster actually brings about a dramatic change in the arena of school organisation.

To organise instructional employees is to win half the objectives of school organisation. Indeed, as an organiser it is the primary duty and responsibility of the headmaster to look into every bit of a problem that the teacher faces inside a class-room or outside it. If he becomes frank enough and easily accessible to the teachers who are not only his colleagues but also partners to academic progress of the school, the smooth organisation of the school as a centre of advancement of learning becomes natural and thrilling. On the other hand, if he unusually maintains some sort of vain prestige and difference from them and wants to show bureaucratic organisational power, the whole purpose of organisation of school as a joint endeavour at devotion to pupil-development in curricular and co-curricular activities related to day to day pursuit of learning is defeated.

The headmaster as an able organiser should also create a favourable and supporting atmosphere for every individual teacher to launch and experiment upon innovative theorises and enrich his educational qualifications and experiences. Much to his disappointment and loss of faith, the teacher interested in progress of learning sometimes faces a passive role of the headmaster pressurized by persons or bodies of vested interests. This should be sternly dealt with by the headmaster as an organising crusader. As he cannot remain a silent spectator of organisational constraints specially in connection with promotion and professional fillip of teachers as his colleagues, he should exercise his organisational leadership to the fullest satisfaction and to the greatest interest and appreciation of the entire educational community.

To look into the organisational role of the teacher inside the class-room is not enough. As education today aims at harmonization of indoor and outdoor activities, the role of the teacher as an educational expert has also undergone a sea-change to explore human resource and potentiality right at the school level. He is engaged in the out-door activities of his pupils to explore newer possibilities of pupil-progress in education. As such, he also takes part in outdoor activities and becomes an inseparable partner to pupil-activities whom he inspires in self activity as an educational organiser. The leadership of the headmaster in this connection is of great importance. As and overall organiser, he also joins hand with the teachers and the pupils in the organisational programmes of outdoor activities.

A recent reference of organisational uniqueness specially with regard to the role of the headmaster and the associated members of the teaching staff of Madhyamgram High School, West Bengal, India in highlighting and fostering the spirit of excellence and glory in the game of football may be appropriate here. Indeed, the school football team has achieved national distinction of outstanding performance more than once and is even now presenting new finds of promising feat.

Admittedly, the relationship between the headmaster and the pupils makes newer inroads in organisation by means of maintenance of harmony and co-operation with teachers in all innovative programmes for implementation curricular or co-curricular.

For a better organisation of school, the headmaster cannot but be well-informative with the advantages the disadvantages of pupils in pursuit of education. As a deviation from the normal role of the headmaster maintaining an undesirable distance between the pupils and himself in school organisation, a continuous and positive rapport between the two not only promotes advancement of learning but also ensures healthy and promising school climate.

The learners who are new entrants in a school demand a shattering of unusual fear and distance between the headmaster and themselves. Again, learners shy or truant need special care and attention, where the headmaster should play a vital role by means of occasional encounter with them. The pupils who are preparing for the final public examination also need the headmaster in the warmth and blessing of his organisation. The latter, by means of arranging special coaching classes for them, for instance, may prove his warmth of love and living touch for these outgoing students. Besides all these special programmes which the headmaster arranges in a well-organised manner in the school, organisation of regular activities for pupils in accordance with the school time-table and inspection of pupils' curricular and co-curricular activities at least at regular intervals bring forth worthy results. Undeniably, the less the distance between the pupils and the headmaster in education, the better is the outcome in the form of all-round development of pupil-personality.

An important aspect of school organisation is to create a healthy atmosphere of mutual understanding and appreciation among headmasters in neighbouring schools. This eliminates the sense of alienation to a great extent and makes a favourable atmosphere for the headmaster to organise effective, dynamic and inter-dependent programmes of school activities. Moreover, with such an organisation of the school, he can efficiently deal with the following problems in school education:

(i) paucity of teachers,
(ii) non-availability of experts in games and sports,
(iii) absence of the school library having necessary books—text or reference ones.
(iv) absence of a well-equipped school laboratory,
(v) absence of necessary gadgets and teaching aids,
(vi) re-orientation programmes for training of teaching personnels,
(vii) change of text-books, incorporation of new matters,

elimination of inappropriate texts, and innovative programmes for acceleration of creative appreciation and critical thinking,

(viii) overhauling evalution programmes in education with particular reference to setting of question papers, examination of answer-scripts, awarding grades/marks, announcing results etc.,

(ix) arranging seminars, workshops, conferences etc. for better organisation and administration of school education.

Admittedly, the suggestions of Education Commission (1964-66) in connection with the school complex for better organisation of the school and the related headmaster's role in each school to efficiently eliminate all types of alienations among teachers, pupils and the community in order to thrust education as an organ for an enlightened humane society are yet to be translated into reality. Even in introducing the *Navodaya Vidyalayas* the objectives of school organisation and the role of the headmaster as an organising leader have not been sufficiently and categorically defined and analysed in terms of the tripartite role of teachers, pupils and the community. It is high time that such organisational clarity of objectives be the guideline for effective school education.

Public relations, consultation with parents/guardians and contact with community representatives have now become inseparable parts of school organisation. As an organising head, the headmaster cannot but maintain cordial relationships with these agencies. He highlights the different aspects of the school before parents/guardians in particular because the parents/guardians are closely concerned with pupils' school education. But the real picture, let us frankly admit, it otherwise, Parents or guardians hardly visit or are invited to visit schools for organisational discussions with the school authorities. Nor are they invited to suggest avenues for improvement of school education. They are normally informed about problems of discipline with regard to their wards or at best of their wards' progress in curricular activities. A well-balanced programme of co-ordination between the school and the parents/guardians or between the school and the community representatives should include the following areas of organisation where the headmaster plays a very key role as an education leader:

(i) to arrange meeting for discussions on diverse issues related to pupil's day to day progress in education.

(ii) to discuss and finalize the planning of the year's work of the school and incorporate invaluable suggestions for progress and development in school education.

(iii) to seek advice and guidance from educational experts and prominent persons engaged in different activities in public and community life.

(iv) to synchronize organisational relationships between the school and the community and chalk out school programmes for involvement in community activities including manual work, nursing the weak and the aged, helping the disabled and the disadvantaged, and participating in community functions and festivals.

(v) to organise the school health programmes by inviting medical experts and acting in accordance with their suggestions.

An important area of organisational activity with which the headmaster cannot but be associated is the role that he plays as a vital linkman with the District School Board, Board of Education, Ministry of Human Resource Development and Ministry of Information and Broadcasting. With his limited role he can maintain closer ties with each of these organisations and seek assistance, suggestions and guidance as and when necessary. Moreover, he can be well-acquainted with the latest trends and tendencies in school organisation by keeping pace with the diverse forms of informatics and resources available or likely to be available in future from these organisations.

The primary task of the headmaster as an organiser is to introduce phased programmes of school activities where every item of activity is caressed and performed by the appropriate application of strategies well-suited to the purpose of completion. A broad-based programme of school organisation designed to synchronize the above end in view may be tabled as follows :

PHASE : 1

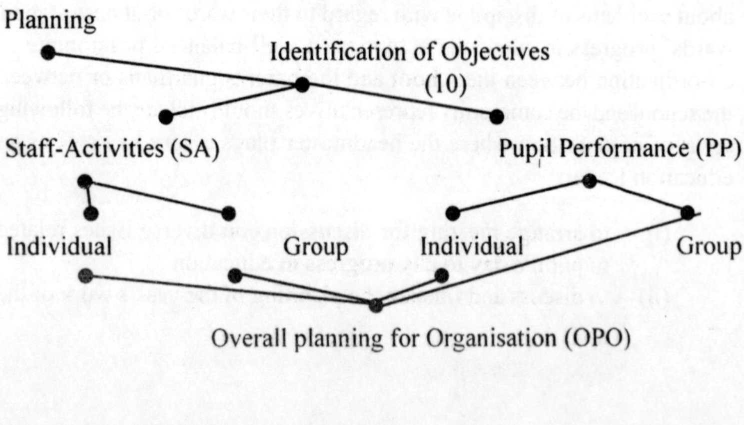

As a key partner in planning, the headmaster is liable to make a cohesion between 10 and its splitters like SA and PP to arrive at a justifiable platform of OPO which is the ultimate goal of phase 1. To organise SA or PP necessitates further spell-out of objectives where the headmaster's suggestions may be of vital importance. Of course, his involvement as an organisational leader in these areas can be made more effective by delegation of organisational leadership to teachers or pupils as and when necessary.

PHASE: 2

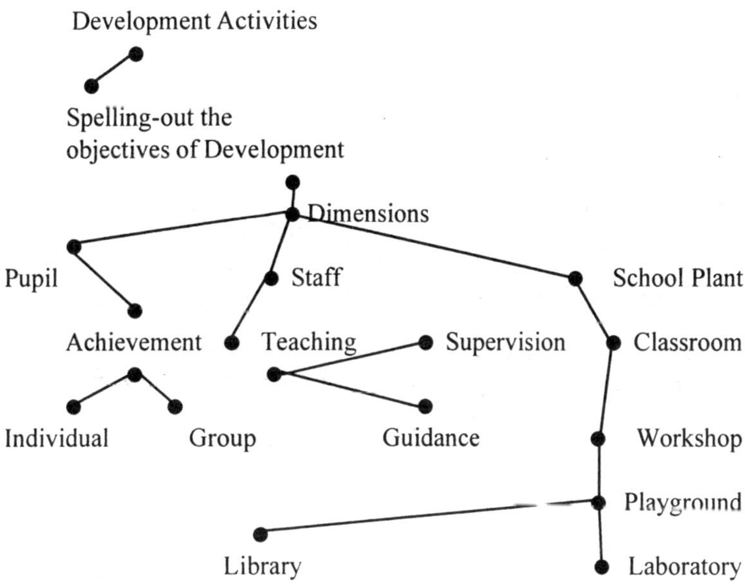

The headmaster's primary involvement in school organisation is with pupils. His organisational leadership begins with a cordial rapport with pupils on the basis of occasional meetings and discussions on different issues and problems on education. His main concern is to identify each of the pupils whose academic performance is not satisfactory and, therefore, needs special instructions in the forms of remediation or further probe for enrichment.

The headmaster also organises remedial programmes of group activities of pupils in consultation with teachers and suggests newer avenues for dynamism and qualitative improvement.

So far as organisation of staff development is concerned, the headmaster gears up his organisational leadership towards improvement of teaching, supervision and guidance. Organisation of orientation courses and workshops for teachers specially designed to qualitative improvement in teaching, supervision and guidance programmes is now raised to the status of efficiency in school leadership. To set a standard of management and control in education, to improvise curriculum and instruction, to monitor communication and progress in education and to timely evaluate learning outcomes of pupils—all come under the domain of organisational leadership where the headmaster always maintains or tries to maintain a balance of diverse activities.

With regard to the school plant, the headmaster as an organiser looks after the problems and possibilities of classrooms, workshops, library, laboratory, playground, school health and sanitation. Even though allocation of duties for these are there, his overall organisational and supervisory suggestions demand a priority. In fact, his occasional show of interest and enquiry, if any, should have a sound basis of organisational breakthrough whenever required. The immediate areas of enquiry encompassing the different components of the school plant, where the headmaster should play his role as an organisational leader are:

(a) Do these promote improvement in education?
(b) Are these in a position to set standards in teaching, guidance and supervision?
(c) Do these act upto the expectations of the pupils, teachers and the community in teaching-learning programmes?
(d) Are these conducive to evaluational programmes from time to time?
(e) Do these support economy of space, time, money and materials?

The headmaster's physical presence in the school sets the whole organisational model in motion. His frequent class-room observations, communications with the members of the teaching and non-teaching staff for academic and administrative clarity of vision and clear-cut, specific and constructive discussion with them for school education are vital to the creation of an agreeable and developmental approach to organisation of education. He knows that improved instructional practice is always an outcome of freedom exercised by teachers as well as pupils devoted to innovative practice in education. He also provides a clear vision of the school in all its programmes of activities, makes newer avenues of research and publication related to education of young learners and sets a thrilling instance of dynamic leadership.

Today's school education is almost entirely dependent on school organisation. If the headmaster as its organisational leader brings about an all-embracing harmonious relationship among teachers, students, parents/guardians and others directly or indirectly associated with different school programmes, he not only succeeds in discharging his duties and responsibilities as a school organiser but also contributes his mite as a nation-builder. Is school organisation really geared to this end-in-view today?

20

SCHOOL ORGANISATION
Future Perspectives

Education is a challenging activity. Organisation of school education is more challenging because it demands a look within in order to bring about a change for the future. Dynamic as every endeavour at organising the school should be, everyone related to school organisation should be imbibed with the spirit of marching on and on in advancement of learning.

To march on and on specially in case of pupils normally encapsulates a pre-condition. It is organisational leadership that comes in the forefront of the fillip to pupil-inspiration and pupil-achievement. Who comes forward to shoulder this organisational leadership in or outside the class-room regularly and directly? The answer, obviously, is the teacher who should hold out the promises of the future before every pupil as best as possible. As a supporting organiser of educational thoughts and experiments the headmaster acts as a kingpin to all plans and programmes encountered now in almost all schools. But even then a gradual and alarming sense of alienation well-visualized from apparent involvements in duties and responsibilities does not avert the eyes of hapless affected pupils. This does need a change. The future teacher and the future headmaster now await the hallowed promise and fulfilment of joint endeavour well-directed towards organising better education for pupils.

How to organise better education? How to improve instruction? How to frame an enlightened and organised curriculum happily wedded to prospective co-curricular activities? How to make an inter-disciplinary approach to education so that education becomes meaningful and a definite pointer to pulsating tomorrows to come in newer avenues of fullness of personality? All these and a host of other questions determine the future perspectives of school organisation.

Modern school organisation has also other parameters related to the following each of which is poignant with future beckonings of advancement of teaching-learning possibilities:

(i) Mini Teaching
(ii) Individualized Instruction
(iii) Mixed Curriculum based on the Inter-disciplinary Approach.
(iv) Superior Aids in Teaching and Pupil-proneness
(v) Creative Thinking and Critical Appreciation

As regards Mini Teaching as an improved strategy for better teaching, organisation of classroom teaching has already undergone ample revision. Re-orientation and revitalisation of Mini Teaching are to be based on the following components with a more scientific and fool-proof endeavour:

(i) Re-organisation of the text-matter suited to the needs and abilities of pupils.
(ii) Qualitative content backed by graded, well–elucidated, sufficiently thought-provoking and dynamic text-matter.
(iii) A balanced and worthy application of aids.
(iv) Better and sufficient individual involvement of the learner.
(v) Application of pin-pointed, natural, easy, spontaneous and endearing stylistics for greater and more penetrating influence upon learners.

Organisation of individualized instruction in school education is crucial to the advancement of better pupil-socialization. Therefore, newer approaches to this direction are not only desirable but also purposeful and meaningful. Improved techniques and strategies for pupil-guidance, use of more reliable, valid and thought-provoking text-books and other materials, and better supervision programmes— all these should enrich future perspectives of school organisation.

A recent trend in school organisation particularly in curriculum reconstruction and curriculum guidance is introduction of Mixed Curriculum based on an Inter-disciplinary Approach. This will certainly eliminate major pitfalls in synchronization of knowledge and experience attained by means of varied endeavour so vital for global socialization of man in organised and well disciplined process of education.

Side by side with introduction of Mixed Curriculum for better school education, a judicious check in the use of teaching aids in order to arrest pupil-proneness to their rampant use thereby making themselves parasites and passive learners, necessitates immediate attention. At the same time, innovative experiments on indigenous teaching aid need a revamping in organisation of school education.

Creative thinking and critical appreciation demand priorities in school education. As such, our future programmes for organisation of education in school should have a special emphasis on this particular end-in-view. Quality in education, indeed, rests on excellence in creativity and critical appreciation. The whole pattern of education in schools demands an extensive overhauling towards this objective which is not yet properly attended to and organised in a well-balanced and systematic way.

School organisation should also be essentially geared to promoting exercise in finer sensibilities and softer visions of life. Mere toying with improved techniques and superior methods in or outside the class-rooms may accelerate pupil-activity and pupil-attention but do not necessarily ensure the ascent and excellence of pupil-personality. In education, what cannot be taught but can alone be *caught* yet remains beyond the purview of organisation. A careful and conscious endeavour at this direction enriches our future perspectives in school organisation. The heartland of educational organisation continually beckons harboring and consolidating education for acceleration of excellence in exercise of aesthetic sensibilities. The taxonomy of school organisation should, therefore, incorporate this essential component of the education of 'being'. Do we respond?

BIBLIOGRAPHY

Aggarwal J.C. and Agrawal, S.P.: *National Policy on Education: Agenda for India 2001*, Concept Publishing Company, New Delhi.

-, -: *Educational Planning in India with a slant to Educational Financing and Administration,* Concept Publishing Company, New Delhi.

Agrawal, B.P and Kanta, Naresh : *Child Education in India*, Concept Publishing Company, New Delhi.

Agrawal, K.P. : *Development of Creativity in Indian Schools,* Concept Publishing Company, New Delhi.

Aldrich, Howard E. : *Organizations and Environments,* Prentice-Hall, Englewood Cliffs, New York, 1979.

Bantock, O. H. : *Freedom and Authority in Education,* Faber & Faber, London, 1953.

Bennis, W. B. : *Changing Organizations*, McGraw-Hill, New York, 1966.

Blackburn, Thomas (Ed.) : *Presenting Poetry*, Methuen, London, 1960.

Chakrabarti, Mohit : *Education for Creative and Aesthetic Consciousness*, Daya Publishing House, Delhi, 1990.

— : *Challenges in Teacher Education*, Daya Publishing House, Delhi, 1993.

— : *Child Education and Creativity*, Daya Publishing House, Delhi, 1994.

Clogg, S. & Dunkerley, D. : *Organisation, Class and Control,* Routledge & Kegan Paul, London, 1980.

Cranston, Maurice, : *Freedom and New Analysis*, Longman, Green & Co. Ltd., London, 1953.

Daft, R. & Becker, S. W. : *The Innovative Organization : Innovation Adoption in School Organization*, Elsener, New York, 1978.

Dewey, John : *How We think,* Heath, Boston, U.S.A. 1933

—: *School and Society*, University of Chicago Press, Chicago, U.S.A. 1943.

Evers, Colin W. and Lakomski, G. : *Knowing Educational Administration,* Pergamon Press, London, 1991.

Etziony, A. : *Modern Organizations*, Prentice-Hall, New York, 1964.
Freeman, Richard : *Mastering Study Skills*, Macmillan, London, 1991.
Fromm, Erich : *Escape from Freodom*, Rinoharb, New York, 1991.
Fullan, M. : *The Meaning of Educational Change,* Teachers' College Press, New York, 1982.
Gandhi, K. L. : *Value Education*, Gyan Books Pvt. Ltd. New Delhi, 1993.
Ghiselin, Brewster (Ed.) : *The Creative Process*, New American Library, New York, 1958.
Gupta, S. S. : *Planning for Academic Excellence,* Concept Publishing Company, New Delhi.
Hage, J. & Aiken, M. : *Social Change in Complex Organizations,* Random House, New York, 1967.
Hammersley, M. & Woods, P. (Eds.) : *The Process of Schooling*, Routledge & Kegan Paul, London, 1976.
Illich, Ivan D. : *Celebration of Awareness : A Call for Instituional Revolution*, Penguin, London, 1974.
King, R. A. : *School Organisation and Pupil Involvement,* Routledge & Kegan Paul, London, 1973.
— : *The Sociology of School Organisation,* Methuen, London, 1983.
McNergney *et al* : *Teacher Development*, Macmillan Publishing Co. Inc. New York, 1981.
Mearns, Hugh : *Creative Power*, Dover Publications, New York, 1959.
Maclure, S. & Davies, P. (Ed.) : *Learning to Think, Thinking to Learn,* Pergamon Press, London, 1991.
Michael, W. B. : *Teaching for Creative Endeavour,* Indian University Press, Bloomington, USA 1988.
Ministry of Education, Government of India : *Challenge of Education : A Policy Perspective*, 1985.
Musgravs. P. W. : *The School as an Organiser*, Macmillan, London, 1990
Nash, Paul : *Authority and Freedom in Education*, John Wiley & Sons Inc. New York, 1966.
Pandey, Janak (Ed.) : *Social Reality : Perspective and Understanding,* Concept Publishing Company, New Delhi.
Pandit Barooah, Pramila : *Handbook on Child : With Historical Background*, Concept Publishing Company, New Delhi.
Reimer, Everett : *School is Dead*, Penguin Books Ltd. London, 1970.
Ross, K. N. & Mahick, L. (Ed.) : *Planning the Quality of Education,* Pergamon Press, London, 1990.
Sinha, Jai B.P. : *School Complex (The) : An Unfinished Experiment*, Concept Publishing Company, New Delhi.
Schmuck, R. & Miles, M. (Ed.) : *Organizational Development in Schools.*

National Press Books, California, U.S.A. 1977.

Silver-Man, D. : *The Theory of Organisations*, Heinemann, London, 1970.

Sinha, Durganand (Ed.) : *Socialisation of the Indian Child,* Concept Publishing Company, New Delhi.

Stephens, T. M. *et al* : *Teaching Mainstreamed Students,* Pergamon Press, London, 1988.

Tagorc, Rabindranath : *Creative Unity, Macmillan*, London, 1962.

Thompson, J. G. : *Organizations in Action*, McGraw-Hill, New York, 1967.

Thompson, V.A. : *Modern Organization*, Knopf, New York, 1961.

Tibble, J. W. (Ed.) : *The Future of Teacher Education,* Routledge & Kegan Paul, London, 1971.

Torrance, E. P. : *Nature of Creative Talent : Theory and Practice*, Prentice-Hall Inc., New York, 1961.

Torrance E.P. : *Rewarding Creative Thinking*, Allyn & Bacon, New York, 1966.

Towards an Enlightened and Humane Society, Commission for Review of National Policy of Education, Ministry of Human Resource Development, New Delhi, 1991.

Tyler, William : *School Organisation : A Sociological Perspective*, Croom Helm Limited, London, 1988.

Vashistha, K. K. : *Teacher Education in India : A Study in New Dimension*, Concept Publishing Company, New Delhi.

Verma, S. L. : *National Information System in Education*, Concept Publishing Company, New Delhi.

White. J. M. & Brewer, N. : *Teaching Basic Skills : The Principles of Instruction*, Macmillan, London, 1993.

INDEX